The
Big Idea
of the
Old Testament

Part 1 in the Foundations of Life Book Series

Derek Mooy

WESTBOW
PRESS°
A DIVISION OF THOMAS NELSON
& ZONDERVAN

WestBow Press books may be ordered through booksellers or by contacting:

WestBow Press
A Division of Thomas Nelson & Zondervan
1663 Liberty Drive
Bloomington, IN 47403
www.westbowpress.com
844-714-3454

ISBN: 979-8-3850-0702-8 (sc)
ISBN: 979-8-3850-0703-5 (hc)
ISBN: 979-8-3850-0704-2 (e)

Library of Congress Control Number: 2023917346

Print information available on the last page.

WestBow Press rev. date: 09/14/2023

Dedication

To Rebekah, with Love.

Grateful.

Contents

Introduction.. ix

Chapter 1: Purpose.. 1
Chapter 2: What's the Big Idea, and Why Do We Need It?................. 9
Chapter 3: What's the Big Idea of the Bible?................................15
Chapter 4: What's the Big Idea of the Old Testament? 19
Chapter 5: What's the Big Idea by Genre? 22
Chapter 6: Law.. 26

                    Genesis.. 32
                    Exodus 37
                    Leviticus 40
                    Numbers 43
                    Deuteronomy 46

Chapter 7: Historical Books 50

                    Joshua 55
                    Judges 58
                    Ruth 63
                    1 and 2 Samuel 68
                    1 and 2 Kings 74
                    1 and 2 Chronicles.. 78
                    Ezra-Nehemiah 82
                    Esther 86

Chapter 8: Wisdom Literature... 91

                    Job 95
                    Psalms..101

Proverbs 108

Ecclesiastes..111

Song of Songs...116

Chapter 9:   Prophets...119

Isaiah 124

Jeremiah... 129

Lamentations 132

Ezekiel 135

Daniel..141

Hosea 146

Joel..149

Amos 153

Obadiah...157

Jonah 160

Micah 164

Nahum 168

Habakkuk..171

Zephaniah 175

Haggai 179

Zechariah.. 184

Malachi... 188

Conclusion 193

Works Cited 195

Introduction

Some things are just not for me to know …

… and that's OK.

It's actually better than OK—it's *really* good. Accepting the truth that we're not geared to handle all the answers of the cosmos is such a weight lifted from one's chest—such a breath of fresh air. Like a beautiful sunrise after a long, dark night, oh how sweet the ability to rest amid the toughest questions of life when you realize it's not your place to understand it all.

Being OK with not knowing the answers to all the deepest questions with which we humans have toiled for centuries is one of the greatest feats we humans can ever accomplish. At least it is for me. But what makes it OK? Why is it acceptable to acknowledge that some things just aren't for us to understand? Is there an "X" factor that grants us authority to rest upon the certainties of life considering the uncertainties? Whether we're dealing with the deep questions of life purely from a philosophical perspective or we're in the trenches of tragedy, what makes it OK to step out into the unknown and simply trust?

I hope you find interest in the same questions upon which I think daily. If so, please continue reading. The introductory chapters of this book serve as an outline of my journey leading to the present day. It is an open book, quite literally and figuratively, to my personal journey. This is where I am at the time of publication. Yet I hope tomorrow's growth leads me to humorously chuckle at the gaps in today's thinking.

While we will deal with the questions of life from a philosophical perspective, let us first deal with the practical side. How do we handle the questions that arise when walking through tragedy? There comes a point in life, or several points if you're anything like most, where you undergo an indescribably dreadful experience. And it's found there during that unspeakable time that you can find legitimate grounds to conclude that the bad simply outweighs the good.

Make no mistake, I'm not about to take you down some dismal path about why life is pointless. There are certainly many reasons to celebrate our existence, and the purpose of this book is to outline the very best of those reasons. We're not going to have any semblance of a victim mentality or allow our mindset to be anything less than one of grit, fortitude, and relentless forward motion. Considering that, I would undoubtedly be remiss to simply invalidate the dark side of life. The side of life that takes you out to the deepest of waters and drowns the very core of your being. The side that is cold, jagged, *unconcerned*. The side that has no regard for the depth at which it cuts you or even the lives it takes. No regard whatsoever for the damage it hurls upon you. Friends, a truly rotten and ruthless side of life *kills all innocence*.

I am not smart enough, enlightened enough, wise enough, or in any other way qualified to provide the *perfect* solution when dealing with problems of this caliber. Even if you and I experience the *same* atrocity, I would still not be able to know exactly how *you* felt or were affected, I would only know how I felt and was affected. However, one thing we humans *can* claim is the authority to sit next to one another in the worst of circumstances and simply be together through it. Good times and bad, just being a presence for one another is sometimes the best and only thing we can offer.

I ask you to take a moment and reflect slowly on the statements below. Think about a time in your life when each applied or currently applies to you. Think of how people appropriately *and* inappropriately tried to help (talked too much versus just sitting in silence). Take your time. Make it personal. Make it deep. Let it in.

Pain … beyond description.

Heartbreak … beyond survivability.

Darkness … beyond *ever* seeing the light.

Hopelessness … beyond despair.

Brokenness … beyond repair.

Shattered … beyond mending.

Ugly … beyond acceptance.

Terrorized … beyond a scream.

Damaged … beyond restoration.

And now imagine each of the above situations as self-induced. This puts a new spin on each of them—it creates a sense of guilt if one allows. It creates a sense of deserving the pain ... deserving of the statement: "To be discarded." It leads one to believe, "I'm not wanted."

And yet, with each of these wrecked situations described above, we all generally want someone to be there for us even in the self-induced cases. There are definitely times when being alone is preferred, but generally, no one wants and certainly doesn't *need* to be alone during the times mentioned above.

So, if this applies to us as individuals, would it not also apply to us as humanity? Would it not be better for someone to come alongside humanity and simply be present?

Just as we individuals have all blown it at times, so too humanity has sorely messed up. As a species we're constantly under the anguish of pain, heartbreak, darkness, hopelessness, brokenness, terror, ugliness, and self-induced damage.

That which once was so beautiful and perfect has fallen. It has fallen into such a state of disarray that to recognize it is to define it as something altogether different than the original. This fallen "something" is called humanity and it brought about this sudden detrimental reversal upon itself—self-induced.

And to simply make a long story short, the unapologetic conclusion we're leading to is this: Someone *has* come to be present. Someone *has* come to be among us ... And it is the Bible that tells the story of this special Someone coming among us and reversing the irreversible. The Bible is the story of God making the impossible, possible. It is the story of God repairing and restoring the broken, shattered, ugly, terrorized, damaged, unrepairable, discarded, self-induced *guilt* of humanity.

We have the official record. The transcript has been given. It is called the Bible. The Bible is God's recorded transcript of His centuries-long process of freeing us from our self-induced hopelessness.

I hope and pray you are uplifted and encouraged by this book. May you lift your eyes and find light at the end of whatever dark tunnel looms in front of you.

For certainly there is light ... Someone has come ... and His torch is bright.

CHAPTER 1

Purpose

So since someone *has* come to deliver us, we should then ask ourselves a very simple question: "Why?" Why would God spend so much time and effort to keep us? What is so worthwhile about us humans that God would go to such great lengths to reconcile us back to Him? What part do we play in His great cosmic plan that makes us worthy of so much sacrifice, work, patience, grace, discipline, and effort on God's part?

At this point we begin delving into questions that no one throughout all time has been able to fully comprehend and exhaustively answer. Therefore, we should tread lightly and walk humbly throughout this process. I'm certainly not going to claim the ability to add to the answer(s) on which the great minds of the past and present have already elaborated.

And yet, while we know we won't be fully satisfying our hunger by explaining the complexity of our purpose, we also don't want to starve ourselves by falling into the common trap of oversimplification. We humans *really* like to understand the intricacies of what makes us who we are. Unfortunately, when we realize we cannot comprehend the fullness of the truth, we're usually willing to dilute it until it becomes comprehensible. You will not find that in this book. This complex question cannot be reconciled with a simplistic answer. That all being said, as far as I can tell, God has made it clear in scripture and in Creation that while *we* are not entirely aware of our full purpose, *God* is. And somewhere in His vast and unlimited mind, He has deemed us and our purpose worth His effort.

The puzzle piece we're on in His great cosmic puzzle is quite important to Him. In the great mind and knowledge of God, He has somehow reconciled that *you are worth it.*

You are enough.

You matter.

You have purpose.

So let us explore this concept of purpose for a moment.

What is purpose? What is the point of existence? And how does this tie into truth?

When one is asked these questions, it could be assumed that one is being asked, "What is the purpose of *my* life?" or "What does truth have to do with *me*?" But to ask any of these questions with "me" in mind starts the journey off altogether on the wrong foot. Conversely, we should initially be more concerned with the purpose of *all* humanity. For it is only within the purpose, point, and truth of all humanity that we can *most accurately* cooperate and contribute individually.

So as we shift from an individual perspective and embark on the journey for humanity's purpose, we must once again pause and zoom out a bit more to determine the purpose of *all life on earth* … and even earth *itself.* But to know the purpose of earth and all its creatures, we must zoom out one more time to assess the purpose of the entire cosmos. This is where it becomes especially problematic, as the cosmos is something so great that we can't even begin to comprehend its size and complexity. Yet we must attempt this—and attempt it we have certainly done. From the dawn of time, we have approached purpose, point, and truth from every imaginable angle. Yet we will bring some simplification to our numerous angles by breaking them down into three separate categories.

First, we humans started off thousands of years ago with religion. Right or wrong, each of these religions granted their adherents some form of purpose, point, and truth by providing answers to the questions that mattered most to each religion's members. In other words, every person or group of people approach the purpose of life with a list of questions that *must* be answered. Whether the questions deal with life after death, bad things happening to good people, the nature of God, or something else, we all search with *big* questions in mind, consciously or subconsciously.

Building on religion, humanity expanded their thought process a bit and began to delve into the category we label philosophy. The word *philosophy* is simply two Greek words smashed together: *philo* meaning *love* and *sophos* meaning *wisdom*. At its core, and extremely oversimplified, philosophy is the love of wisdom. Since the dawn of philosophy proper, it and religion have worked in tandem to help each other sort out the questions of life. Many people believe religion and philosophy are at constant odds with each other, and sometimes they certainly are. But overall, they have heavily influenced each other throughout the centuries with a sort of back-and-forth dialogue pointing out each other's weaknesses. The result is that they are both more formidable in grappling with the questions of life.

The last category with which we humans have recently engaged to answer questions of purpose, point, and truth is science. Like religion and philosophy, science has stepped in to add another positive layer of filtration to our understanding. Again, many folks are under the impression that science is at odds with religion and sometimes philosophy, but I take a completely different approach. Science is not at odds with God, for *true* science is simply humanity's explanation of what God has done. So again, science is not at odds with God; rather it is people's preconceived notions about science that are at odds with Him. Any scientific opinion that leads to an atheistic conclusion has been propagated by folks who have simply set out to prove their predetermined ideology. This is confirmation bias at its worst. It is the injected poison of subjectivity into what is supposed to be an objective process. It is the ridiculous development of data that points to one's already-held beliefs instead of simply letting the data lead to its own conclusions. Covering this perspective in depth is not the purpose of this book, but we must address it at a surface level.

Science cannot ever in any way answer the question of *purpose* like religion or philosophy can, but it does grapple with *truth* in a way that religion and philosophy simply are not equipped to do. In essence, science explains why things are the way they are in this physical world. But science cannot bestow purpose beyond the physical description. So again, I believe that religion, philosophy, *and* science team up in a unity that undoubtedly broadens our knowledge in a way that each could not do alone.

Since the relationship between religion and science is quite a hotly debated topic, let's develop my statements above just a bit more. While we should make every attempt to approach the quest for truth with an open, unbiased mind, no one is fully exempt from approaching science and other methods of truth-seeking without preconceived notions of truth. Some approach science from an atheistic perspective, which leads to the conclusion, "Ha! I'm right after all! There is no God!" On the contrary, others look at the same science and stand in awe with the conclusion "Oh my goodness! God sure is amazing!" In other words, while science is great at presenting theories and facts regarding this physical world, it is also *strangely geared* to participate in our own individual confirmation biases regarding our spiritual beliefs. For this reason, the staunch atheist must be aware that science just simply isn't outfitted to explain anything beyond the physical cosmos. Likewise, people of faith must also be aware that science does not always have to support our scriptures, as they were not intended to provide a scientific model of the universe. Science deals with the physical world, and the Bible deals with the spiritual world. As Jaroslav Pelikan states:

> The Bible is not intended to be a universal history of the whole human race, much less a cosmogony that accounts for the structure and laws of the entire physical and biological universe ... Rather, the Bible consistently directs our attention away from cosmogony, ... the special relation between God and the human race.[1]

We as Christians must understand that our Bible was not intended to give us answers to the physical nature of our existence. Likewise, people believing only in science cannot broach questions that must be analyzed outside the scientific method and the five senses. Religion, philosophy, and science help one another, but they cannot definitively answer one another's questions. (This is a very serious oversimplification, but please understand this is not a position paper on the relationship between religion, philosophy, and science. Many others far better at this than I have already done this.)

All this being said, let's go back to the beginning. Finding our individual purpose, point, and truth must be determined within the context of all humanity. But humanity's purpose must be established within the context of the whole earth. Then again, to define earth's purpose, we must look

---

[1] Jaroslav Pelican, *Whose Bible Is It? A History of the Scriptures Through the Ages* (New York: Viking Penguin, a member of Penguin Group (USA), 2005), 29.

another layer deeper within the context of the entire cosmos. So how can we even begin to grasp all this purpose, point, and truth? Science can only explain *physical* truth, but we cannot look to scientifically provided models to determine purpose. Philosophy can provide answers in several legitimate and illegitimate ways dependent on the starting assumptions, but this book is more geared toward religion, specifically Christianity. Therefore, we will simply have to bow out gracefully to any in-depth conversation on the vast and varied philosophical stances. Our discussion will focus on religion, but we would be wise to keep in mind that science and philosophy are always on standby, waiting to check religions' conclusions. In essence, we acknowledge the credibility of science and philosophy, but we are focusing our discussion on the ability of religion to provide purpose.

To recap our discussion earlier on purpose, ultimately we find our purpose as humanity and as individuals within the context of the encompassing purpose of the entire cosmos. This means that we must first know the purpose of the cosmos before we can determine our own purpose within it. And as with all things created, whether it be a building, a fence, computer software, or a garden, the most qualified individual to clarify purpose is its creator. This is where religion truly shines, as it assumes the cosmos was created with intelligent design.

So now we're left with only one last step in determining our purpose … we make the *ever so scandalous attempt* to peer into the abyss of the cosmos and kindly ask for a conversation with its Creator. We do this to determine the purpose of the Creation as dictated by the Creator.

So, let's assume for a moment that we humans have absolutely no knowledge of this Creator. There are no religions to teach us truth, no holy books, no defined ideas of the characteristics of a Designer … we have nothing solid upon which to base our understanding. The only thing we know for certain is that we were created. How would you come to know what this Creator is like? How would you determine how you are to interact with this Creator, if at all? How would you verify this Creator's expectations? Ultimately, how would you determine your purpose, point, and truth in relation to your newfound knowledge that there is an Intelligent Designer of the cosmos?

Unquestionably, you can look around and see tremendous amounts of organization in the beauty of the cosmos which makes the belief in a

Creator a reasonable conclusion. But does this teach you anything *specific* about the Creator? No, it *plainly* does not. Observing nature absolutely confirms a Creator (Romans 1) but it teaches us nothing regarding this Creator's specifics ... *and this is a problem*. It is a *big* problem because if you buy into my line of thinking with the thought experiment we're currently conducting, we must first know the purpose, point, and truth *as dictated by the Designer* before we can drop ourselves into it and find our own little part ... In other words, we must first get to know at least a few specifics regarding the nature of the Creator before we can begin to understand the intent of the Creator's purpose in creating us! So what do we do?

Science can only explain our physical world *as understood by the human intellect*, but it cannot see beyond our physical reality to decipher its purpose. To put it another way, science explains *how* things work but not *why* things work. Similarly, the ultimate foundation of philosophy is also the human intellect, logic, and reason. But as we all know too well, our intellect can take us only so far. What are we to do about this dilemma? Both science and philosophy have a *big* problem in that they rely *exclusively* on human intellect and observational authority. Therefore, while this is *not* an argument for the "God of the gaps" theory, we do have to admit that since the authority of science rests merely upon human ability, it will certainly prove to be incompetent in answering the big questions of life. At the end of the day, without some sort of external intervention from this Creator, we are left floating in the emptiness of space chasing our tail. The only thing we can do is throw ourselves at the mercy of this Designer and take what we are given. Good, bad, or ugly ... we are at the hands and will of the information with which this Designer decides to provide us. We have no say in what we receive or how it is received. We are simply tasked with taking it or leaving it.

To a Christian, this is where the Bible comes into play. The Bible is the collection of information that this Creator has decided to give humanity. It is everything God wants us to use as our base in determining our purpose, point, and truth. The Bible doesn't just simply contain *truths* about God, but it is *the* truth about God. Although it doesn't reveal to us absolutely everything about God, it does reveal *everything He determined we need to know*. With that in mind, what does this Bible teach us about God and the ways in which we are to interact with Him?

To list a few, without the Bible we would know nothing of our own fallen state, of God's plan to rescue us, or of how we are to approach God and His people. To put it quite simply, without God formally educating us about Himself (the Bible), we would have no solid foundation upon which to base our understanding of Him. Afterall, the ultimate purpose of the Bible is to provide an accurate revelation not of ourselves but of God.

Before we move on, a brief note must be made. (This note is only intended to be an extreme overview and certainly an oversimplification, but the point still needs to be made.) The above information explaining the need for God to provide the Bible can be used by any religion to support its claim to their holy book's authority. This is so important to understand because unfortunately in our society today when two religions are debating, they tend to use the same arguments to back up the authority of their holy books. In other words, the entire argument above for why God needed to intervene and give us the Bible can also be used by Muslims to explain why Allah gave them the Koran ... or why the Baha'i have the Seven Valleys and the Four Valleys ... or why Hinduism has the Vedas ... or why Judaism has the Tanakh and the Talmud, etc. So it doesn't matter if you're arguing for the Bible as the Word of God or any other religion's holy scriptures as the Word of God, the above argument can be used for them all. Why is this important? Well, it helps us to take a brief pause and best understand the point of this book. This book is not being written as an apologetic or defense of the Christian faith. As a matter of fact, there are so many statements above in this introduction that have probably created so much psychological noise to critical thinkers on both sides of the aisle. This is intentional as I am simply making truth claims and moving on for the sake of clarity as the line of thought is being conveyed. So, this book assumes its readers agree that the Bible is the Word of God ... or at least that they are open to the idea. If you're a Christian seeking to better understand the Bible, this book is for you. Likewise, if you are trying to gain better sense of the Bible to help you determine if you believe it or not, this book is also and most certainly for you. However, if you are looking for a defense of the Christian faith ... well, far greater minds than I have dealt with this topic in hundreds and possibly thousands of books in far better ways than what I would ever be able to provide.

The purpose of this book is to help the Christian and the seeker of truth better understand God's Word, specifically the Old Testament. We will accomplish this by starting with the big picture of the Bible as a whole and gradually zoom in on each individual book.

The only hope I have in writing this book is that you will draw closer to our great Creator, Sustainer and Provider of all life. The hope is that it will ultimately place more feet on the floors of Heaven through the work of Jesus Christ.

Be encouraged by it. Be corrected by it. Be blessed by it. Know God by it.

CHAPTER 2

What's the Big Idea, and Why Do We Need It?

As we approach God's Word, we are to do so with utter humility and admiration. We come to the Bible not with our agenda; rather, we come to it seeking the agenda of the Almighty. In complete opposition to current Western culture and worldview, we would be wise to realize that Universal Absolute Truth *does* exist and is *not* something contained within us or to be determined by us. Rather, it is something external and separate from us. This *external* essence called Absolute Truth has been prepared for us to hunt, gather, ingest, absorb, and metabolize *internally*. In other words, no one can define their own truth. This is in 100 percent conflict with the teaching of modern culture that states we all define our own truth.

This false idea that "what's true for you isn't true for me" or "what's wrong for you isn't wrong for me" bombards even the church world today. With regard to false biblical interpretation, this false ideology has cloaked itself in statements such as "what this verse means to me is ..." or "what God is saying to me through this verse is ..." We've all heard people make statements like this—matter of fact, *most of us* have done it. And while the intention is pure and good the theology is not. A serious student of God's Word must quickly abandon this philosophy of determining what God's Word means to "me" and rephrase the question to something like: "What does God want to communicate to me?" You see, to pose the question as "What this means to *me*?" is to ask the wrong question entirely. So, we take the statement "What this passage means to me?" and reconstruct it in the form of a question: "What does God want to communicate to me?" or "What does this verse mean *FOR* me?" To some folks, this discussion on semantics seems pointless, but by rephrasing the question we are taking the first step in the long, arduous journey of removing the subjective personal opinion of interpreting scripture. This is one of the keys to possessing a more accurate understanding of scripture.

So how does the rephrasing of the question bring us to a clearer understanding? Well, if any given scripture has a certain meaning to you but something entirely different to me, who is correct? Can we both be correct? Or to ask the question a different way, can a single scripture have multiple meanings dependent upon the reader? The short answer is absolutely and *always* no! Please, please, please take this to heart! Scripture means what it means regardless of the reader, their situation, or the metaphorical lens through which they interpret any given passage. We must take this approach if we want to come to any sort of accuracy in what God is communicating. But … if we do not take this approach we will undoubtedly "put in" a different meaning each time we read it versus "pulling out" God's intended meaning. If you spend much time at all studying this concept, you'll run into a few words describing this phenomenon. The first word, *exegesis*, is the proper way to handle scripture and can be summarized as "pulling from" scripture what is actually there. In contrast, the incorrect way to handle scripture is known as eisegesis and is briefly described as "putting into" scripture a message that is simply not there. And before you say you never do the latter, please take note that we have *all* done it from time to time. This is not a time for anyone reading this to feel exempt. As with all aspects of life, those that think they are the least affected are usually most affected. (Side note: do a quick study on the Dunning-Kruger Effect).

God is the author of scripture, but He used humans to write the original autographs. (The term *autograph* is used to describe the original document penned by the author while the term *manuscript* is used to refer to the copies written in their original languages we have today). While the original scriptures (autographs) were written *for* us, they were not originally written *to* us. This is an important distinction to understand. The scriptures were first written to people other than us, and these original audiences lived in different cultures, times, and circumstances. The scriptures were originally written to address these people of long ago in their setting.

Without you and I knowing why the original author wrote to the original audience, we will 100 percent read into scripture something that is simply not there. We unintentionally tend to read into scripture our own circumstances and thus derive an incorrect meaning.

Let me illustrate this point. There has been a time when you've been sick with a stomachache, sore back, headache, shoulder pain, etc. and discussed your symptoms with a friend only to have them diagnose you with absolute certainty. We've all been there. Usually somewhere in the diagnosis they elaborate on how they had the same exact thing, and that's how they knew what was wrong. In reality, a cough or sore stomach can have hundreds of causes, but your friend diagnosed you through the lens of his or her own experience. That person was "putting into" your diagnosis something that was probably not there (eisegesis) instead of "pulling from" what was actually there (exegesis) to provide a proper diagnosis as would a doctor.

Let me illustrate this another way. We've all vented to a friend regarding the check engine light on our vehicle and the subsequent problems it was having. Many times, that friend will say something like, "Oh, I bet I know the problem ... I had this car once that did the same thing and this was the issue ..." Again, most of the time he or she is looking through the lens of personal experience, which causes him or her to misdiagnose your dilemma.

We do the same thing with scripture.

We read a passage with our own circumstances in mind and misdiagnose the meaning. This is why it is 100 percent unequivocally vital to first set aside our perspective and circumstances (as best as we can) and determine the original intent to the original recipient. We must first understand the intent from the biblical author to the original audience before we can begin to apply it correctly into our lives.

Another way of looking at this is the difference between a liberal versus conservative understanding of literary interpretation, biblical literature included. A more liberal perspective states that the meaning of any given text, poem, novel, etc. is dependent upon the reader. In other words, the author's original intent is not given near as much credibility as the current reader. In modern collegiate literature classes, this perspective pervades the classroom—the student determines the meaning of great classical works. How can this be true? Where have we become so arrogant to give a meaning to Shakespeare's great works that Mr. Shakespeare himself never intended?

In contrast, the conservative perspective states that to properly understand any piece of literature, including the Bible, we *must* have a solid understanding of the *original intent* of the *original author* as communicated to the *original audience.* The only individual qualified to define meaning and interpretation to the great works of Hamlet or Romeo and Juliet is the author, William Shakespeare. To think that these great works are defined by the modern reader is absurd and profusely arrogant. The same is true for scripture: the meaning is not determined by the modern reader, and to think otherwise is either unwieldly prideful or recklessly uninformed. Therefore, this book falls strictly and unapologetically into this conservative perspective that scripture means to us only what it meant to the original audience. So, to sum up the philosophical perspective of this book:

Before we can know what the scripture means to us, we must first know what it meant to the original recipients. It cannot mean to us something different than what it meant to the original audience. The Bible must be understood through the lens of the original audience's perspective, not our twenty-first century perspective.

The three preceding sentences may be the most important statements in this entire book! Everything you will read here, including our definition of the Big Idea of the Bible, is founded upon this philosophy! As the theologian C. Hassell Bullock puts it: "Since biblical theology, in our view, must explain what the text meant to its ancient hearers and what it means to us today, we shall in turn address ourselves to both questions."[2] Gaining understanding of scripture with this philosophy as our starting point is extremely critical because the meaning we derive from scripture will dictate how we apply it into our lives!

So, if knowing the original meaning as intended by the original author to the original recipients is so vital, how do we determine it? Well, we

---

[2] C. Hassell Bullock, *An Introduction to the Old Testament Poetic Books* (Chicago: Moody, 1979, 1988), 2.

simply start with the Big Idea and work our way down to the individual words and phrases. The Big Idea does this by taking the following stance:

Before we can understand a phrase or word in the Bible, we must first understand the context within which the word or phrase is used; that is, we must understand the point of the verse within which it is found.

Before we can understand the verse, we must first understand the passage within which it is found.

Before we can understand the passage, we must first understand the book.

Before we can understand the book, we must first understand the genre.

Before we can understand the genre, we must first understand the testament.

And finally, before we can understand the testament, we must first understand the main point of the Bible.

So, in essence, before we can properly understand and apply the individual words and phrases, we must first have a good grasp on the single main point of the entire Bible. Not only does each book have a Big Idea, but each of those Big Ideas must be in harmony with the Big Idea of the Bible as a whole! The smaller units must fit within the context of the larger units. As David M. Howard Jr. states: "It is in the details, as well as in the large-scale sweeps, that we learn about the messages of the biblical books and, ultimately, about God."[3]

Let's use an example from the workplace to illustrate this Big Idea concept. There have been so many times when I have received instructions on a project at work that made absolutely no sense to me whatsoever. Yet when my boss took the time to explain the bigger picture, my little part made sense. In the same way, there have been countless times when I was the one giving orders ... only to receive the same blank stare of confusion in return. However, after I explained the bigger picture, the details made more sense. Have you been there? Have you received directions that made no sense until you were explained the end goal? In the same way, we must understand the Big Idea of scripture to best understand and apply the details.

---

[3] David M. Howard Jr., *An Introduction to the Old Testament Historical Books* (Chicago: Moody, 1993), 24.

As we delve into the Old Testament, we're not going to be breaking down Hebrew sentence structures or doing major word studies. Rather, the intention of this book *is to properly equip the reader with a solid grasp on the Big Idea of the Bible, then the testament, followed by genre, and concluding with each book.* This will hopefully add a few tools to your toolbox to make you better equipped to follow the trickle-down effect from the Big Idea of the Bible all the way to the words and phrases on your own. Therefore, this book is not intended to be a commentary but rather a guide to assist those who are willing to take these concepts further and dig deep beyond what is presented herein.

CHAPTER 3

What's the Big Idea of the Bible?

While we've spent only a short bit of time in the introduction establishing why God gave us His Word, we should understand that numerous books have been written on the topic. I would encourage you to delve into the literature and submerse yourself. You'll never find its end. And while it is necessary to continue scholarship in this area with even more books written on the purpose of the Bible, the end goal of the unlimited supply of books should be to help us formulate *a single sentence* describing the purpose of God's Word. In other words, the thousands of books should all be used to help us bring such a sharp clarity to the purpose of scripture that we can explain it to a first-grader. The millions of words contained within the thousands of books should provide a context within which we can accurately define the purpose of the Bible in one sentence. But why? A single sentence is much more difficult to formulate, as each word must be meticulously scrutinized. However, this single sentence can also be a much stronger hinge upon which we hang our remaining interpretive skills, *if it truly represents the overall main purpose.* Books on the topic are wonderful. I have read several in preparation for *this* book. Bullet points are also wonderful as you are not tasked with encapsulating the entirety of the Bible's purpose in one statement. However, the clarity brought about by a single sentence simply cannot be matched.

When I was a student at Southwestern Assemblies of God University, our biblical interpretation and preaching professors required that we be able to sum up each sermon in a single sentence. While our sermons had more than one point, each of those points were required to support that one-liner. We are simply trying to do the same thing when we build our Big Idea of the Bible. Though the Bible communicates several points, each point in a direct or indirect way should tie back into the foundation of the Big Idea.

Another way to illustrate this is by looking back at our elementary school days. We all learned this "Big Idea" concept in grade school as we began to expand our sentences into paragraphs. Think back to when you were first tasked with writing a paragraph. I specifically remember being overwhelmed. But my teacher took the class through the process that included a main sentence followed by supporting sentences and then ended with a concluding sentence that tied everything back together. The paragraph's concluding sentence really isn't much different than what we are doing when we formulate a single sentence that describes the purpose of the Bible.

A huge word of caution must be pointed out. There is a *major* downfall in attempting to describe the Bible in a single sentence—so much so that some theologians refuse the task altogether. In contrast, the reason we *are* going to attempt to state the purpose of the Bible in a single sentence is to bring clarity to the student of God's Word. However, what if that single sentence doesn't fully capture the Bible's full purpose? What if it is exclusive to certain themes we find in scripture? At this point the simplification provided through the single sentence can lead us to less understanding of God's Word. It weakens the foundation—and this is deadly. This Bible we read is so multifaceted and intricate that condensing it down to a single sentence is an attempt, in the opinion of some, to oversimplify God's purpose. Therefore, we must tread lightly and think deeply if we are to do this.

So, what is the single sentence that carves out the meaning and purpose of the Bible. Well, that's where this becomes difficult for me as I heed to warnings of those smarter than I. As a matter of fact, I will have to contradict myself and give a few different sentences. But don't worry, I'll follow them up by clarifying the single sentence I personally choose to use in my own study.

First, we can look at the Bible itself for a very solid and inspired single sentence. That sentence is found in 2 Timothy 3:16–17 and it reads like this in the New International Version:

> All Scripture is God-breathed and is useful for teaching, rebuking, correcting, and training in righteousness, so that the man of God may be thoroughly equipped for every good work.

You can't really get much better than quoting scripture itself. These are the very words of God telling us the purpose of scripture. But let's also look at another possible Big Idea before following it up with my personal choice.

"The whole point of the Bible, 'the Word of God' on paper, is to reveal and lead us to Christ, 'the Word of God' in human flesh."[4]

This definition as well as the quote from 2 Timothy are outstanding ways to describe the Big Idea of scripture! In line with these, the sentence below is what we will use as our Big Idea of the Bible as we work through the thought process in this book:

The Bible is God's revelation of Himself, ultimately pointing us to Jesus Christ, and teaches us how we are to have proper relationship with Him and His people.

In a single sentence, we've decided on the Big Idea of the Bible. Admittedly, I am personally nervous to make this attempt as we are dealing with God's Word—we *do not* want to lose *meaning* in our attempt to bring *clarification*. We tread lightly as we want to be sure it is inclusive of all God intended to communicate through His Word. Lord, please forgive me where I fall short.

As of today, the definition above is my personal definition of the Big Idea of the Bible. However, I am perfectly comfortable if you disagree because I could be wrong. God gave us the Bible so that we could know Him through His Son Jesus Christ. Yet, for as many days as the Good Lord gives me on this earth, I will always be willing and intentionally searching for a more clarifying statement. I encourage you to do the same.

That being said, the Big Idea of the Bible, as provided above, will serve

---

[4] Peter Kreeft and Ronald Tacelli, *Pocket Handbook of Christian Apologetics* (Westmont: Intervarsity Press, 2003), 82.

as the entire foundation for all else that follows. I pray with bended knee to Jesus Christ that it will suffice.

A final note: I don't blame you if you are not comfortable identifying a single sentence to reflect the purpose of the Bible. One way to reframe this is to define reasons to read the Bible. Why do we study it? Why do we read it? Why do we meditate on it? According to one theologian, three reasons exist: "to discover its revelation of God to us, to learn of His gracious plan of redemption, and to discern how to live."[5]

---

[5] David M. Howard Jr. *An Introduction to the Old Testament Historical Books.* (Chicago: Moody, 1993), 58.

CHAPTER 4

What's the Big Idea of the Old Testament?

It is somewhat of a common misconception that God deactivated his work during the intertestamental period—the four hundred years between Malachi and Jesus. In contrast, God was diligently directing the outcome of human history just as attentively as He did during the Old and New Testaments. As a matter of fact, so much influential activity took place during this intertestamental period that theologians by the droves have focused their life's research and contributions to this period.

But what does this have to do with the Big Idea of the Old Testament? The answer to this is quite simple. At its core, the Bible is separated into two testaments for a couple of reasons. The main reason we will discuss is the natural break in time between the prophets and the coming of Jesus. Clearly a new era had begun with the arrival of the Messiah, so it seems like a natural point to "start a new chapter." Yet what this causes sometimes is a tendency to view the Old Testament as something separate, irrelevant, stale, overworked, tired, worn out, ragged, and ready to be set aside. Oh my … how wrong we humans can be! Though the Old Testament does not record the ultimate fulfillment of our salvation by presenting Jesus Christ, it unequivocally sets the stage for this world-changing event. In other words, the Old Testament and the New Testament do the same thing—they present "Act 1" and "Act 2" of humanity's rescue.

The Old Testament is the *legitimizing ground* of the New Testament.

Without it, the New Testament would make absolutely no sense—historically or theologically. Therefore, the Old Testament is the story of how God set the stage to bring about the Messiah — Jesus Christ. It is the "Act 1" of God rescuing us from ourselves!

Arriving at a central theme for something as large and intricate as the Old Testament is quite an undertaking. While some theologians don't make the attempt, Paul House, in his book *Old Testament Theology*, sums it up quite clearly:

> Despite the current reluctance among some scholars to adopt a single centering theme, Old Testament theology needs focal points. The key here is to argue for a main focal point, not necessarily for the central theme of the Old Testament.[6]

Please remember the points made in the previous chapter:

Using a single sentence to sum up the point of the Bible (the Old Testament in this case) is done for the purpose of bringing clarity. A single sentence is much easier to internalize than a paragraph or list of bullet points.

We must be *extremely* careful when attempting to encapsulate the purpose of the Old Testament in a single sentence. It is very likely that the constraints of a single sentence will not provide room enough to truly represent the full purpose of such a large body of writing.

So, with the warnings above, the single sentence this book will use as a foundation for the purpose of the Old Testament is:

The Old Testament is the theological foundation and historical record upon which our knowledge of God <u>and</u> the coming of Jesus Christ rests.

Let's break this down. The first requirement of the Big Idea of the Old Testament is that it reinforces and supports the Big Idea of the Bible as a whole. We defined the Big Idea of the Bible in the previous chapter as: "The Bible is God's revelation of Himself, ultimately pointing us to Jesus Christ, and teaches us how we are to have proper relationship with Him and His people." With this in mind, it seems fair to state that the

---

[6] Paul R. House, *Old Testament Theology* (Downers Grove, IL: Intervarsity Press, 1998), 56.

Big Idea of the Old Testament falls into submission and agreement with that of the whole Bible.

After ensuring that the smaller piece confirms the whole (i.e., the Old Testament confirms, agrees with, and supports the entire Bible), we then move on to the next requirement. We do this by asking the question: "Does our Big Idea of the Old Testament exclude anything vital to its character and message?" In other words, does our Big Idea do a good job of representing the Old Testament, or is it missing something? This is the most difficult requirement. As previously stated, this is so difficult that many theologians refuse to attempt it—and they have good reason. We won't spend much time here discussing why because it's already been discussed earlier. Suffice it to say that we must remain *absolutely humble* with our determination of the Big Idea of the Bible and of the Old Testament for two reasons:

1. The remaining chapters of the book hinge on these two statements. If these Big Ideas are incorrect or exclusive to an essential aspect of the Bible or Old Testament's purpose, then our starting premises are wrong. If our starting premises are wrong, then our conclusions will be as well.
2. It's incredibly difficult to encapsulate the entirety of the Bible and/or Old Testament in a single sentence, and we certainly do not want to exclude anything God intended to communicate.

That all being said, after significant research and development on this Big Idea, my current position is that it is correct. Please be sure to test it for yourself and if it proves to be lacking, please contact me so we can discuss. If I am wrong, I beg the Lord's forgiveness ... and yours as well. Representing God's Word bears the weight of incredible responsibility, humility, and diligence, so I am serious when I say please contact me if you see error in my judgment.

CHAPTER 5

What's the Big Idea by Genre?

The student of God's Word is typically well aware of the different books and testaments, but many are not as familiar with the role of genre. However, as one begins to grapple with specific genres of biblical literature, he or she begins to progress toward a better understanding of biblical interpretation. This is often one of the watershed moments when believers take their study *and their life* to another level as it results in a more accurate interpretation of scripture. And when one better understands scripture, he or she can better apply it.

So, if genre is so important, what is it? The Merriam-Webster Dictionary defines genre as: "1: A category of artistic, musical, or literary composition characterized by a particular style, form, or content; 2: kind, sort."[7] In other words, there are various kinds of art, music, and literature.

The genres of art are numerous: abstract, architecture, photography, sculpture, Renaissance, modern, etc. Each of these genres have their own purpose and method of conveying their message. Renaissance art and abstract art cannot be viewed through the same lens because they are completely different styles that require different interpretive means.

Music is no different: rock & roll, opera, country, pop, symphony, Christian, etc. Each of these can be divided into further subgenres, but just by looking at a few of the main categories it can be clearly seen that different styles of music are to be understood in different and unique ways.

---

[7] "Genre." *Merriam-Webster.com Dictionary*, Merriam-Webster, https://www. merriam-webster.com/dictionary/genre. Accessed 1 Jun. 2021.

Similarly, if art and music are naturally divided into different genres that come with their own set of interpretive rules, it is only natural to believe the same for literature. This also includes the different styles of literature found within God's Holy Word. While there are many genres and subgenres found within literature, we will stick to just a few that comprise most of scripture: poetry, prose, and letter. There will be more said later with regard to the different interpretive methods for each genre.

As Christians, we do not negotiate when we make the claim that God is absolutely and unequivocally the author of the Bible. When we say that God inspired the Bible, we mean that when it is read, we can rest assured that we are reading exactly what God intended. Therefore, with God as the True Author, He decided to use human beings to do the actual physical writing of His message. This is where it gets interesting. As God inspired different people to pen different books of the Bible, He allowed their different personalities, vocabularies, and writing styles to show up in the writing.[8]

For example, King David wrote many of the Psalms and did so in the form, or genre, of poetry and song. He was a musician, and so he simply wrote songs and poems using his God-given abilities. Contrast this with Paul's writing in the New Testament, and we encounter an entirely different creature. Paul wrote letters to different churches that were formatted according to the standard letter of his day. He started with an introduction and followed it with the body of the letter and a conclusion/salutation. How different this is to David's poetry one thousand years prior!

We can take this a step further and compare Paul's vocabulary to that of Peter or John. Paul was a highly educated man who touted a large and "churchy" Greek vocabulary filled with "larger-than-life" words. Some of his language was rarely or never used by the common folk of his day. This is illustrated by the fact that Paul used several words in the New Testament writings that no other biblical writer used. In contrast, Peter and John used

---

[8] Dozens upon dozens of books have been written on this topic over the course of hundreds of years. I almost included a chapter on this concept but chose not to as it goes beyond the purpose of this book. I encourage you to study this concept more thoroughly. F. F. Bruce is a highly credible theologian who has written extensively on the topic.

a much more common, everyday, "working man's" vocabulary known as *koine* Greek, derived from the influence of the Roman Empire as it spread under the reign of Alexander the Great.[9] Paul was highly educated by the most respected church leader of his day and was equipped with a vocabulary stout enough for the most rigorous of theological discussions. Conversely, Peter and John were fishermen accustomed to the vocabulary required to pull in a net of fish or navigate a boat on rough waters. The neat thing about this is that *God allowed these differences to show forth in each of their writing styles.*

Differences in Interpreting Poetry, Prose, and Letters

Due to different genres contained within scripture, we simply cannot interpret every verse, passage, or book of the Bible the same way *while still properly understanding God's intended message.* For example, when interpreting Moses's writings, we use, for the most part, a literal approach. In other words, when God called Abram up from the land of Ur, we believe Abram *literally* left Ur and went north to Haran just as scripture tells us in Genesis 12. When God gave Moses the Ten Commandments in Exodus 20, we believe that we are *literally* supposed to keep God first and refrain from lying and murdering. However, when we approach some of the Psalms, we cannot interpret that poetry with the same literal mindset with which we approach Moses's prose. Psalm 18:2 states "God is my Rock, my fortress and my Deliverer; my God is my Rock in whom I take refuge, my shield and the horn of my salvation, my stronghold." If we approach the Psalms the same way we approach some of Moses's writings then we have to conclude that Psalm 18 is teaching us that God is a rock and a horn. But we all know, by means of common sense, that David was identifying God as our Strong Protector with use of metaphor. So why couldn't he have just said "God is my Protector"? David was expressing himself through the genre of poetry using imagery, metaphors, and a host of other literary devices just like modern poetry/music—so we must approach the Psalms with that in mind.

---

[9] V. Bubenik. "The Rise of Koine." In *A History of Ancient Greek: From the Beginnings to Late Antiquity.* A. F. Christidis, ed. (Cambridge: University Press), 342–45.

We all understand that King David calling God a rock is obviously not to be taken literally—he was using metaphor just as did Bob Seger when he penned the song "Like a Rock." Yet, this example serves in making the point that not all scripture was intended to be understood as literal—we must find God's purpose in giving us each of the genres of scripture if we are to best understand and apply its meaning. This requires us to bring a well-rounded arsenal of interpretive skills to the table and allow God to direct us just as He directed the biblical authors. God directed the biblical authors in *writing* the scripture (we call this revelation) and now He also directs us in *understanding* the scripture (we call this illumination).

Theologians have categorized genres differently, but most of them fall within somewhat of a similar framework. For the purposes of this book, the genres of the Old Testament will be understood as: law, historical books, wisdom literature, and prophets.

Though there are other ways to categorize the Old Testament books, this categorization will suit our needs. Remember, our goal is to structure the genres in such a way that we can look at each genre and say that "as a very general rule, this is how we are to approach and interpret these books." The list we're using provides us with the most basic structure that still allows for clearly delineating different interpretive methods for each genre, generally speaking.

Just for information's sake, other categories and subcategories or genres you could use to further break down the Old Testament include: major prophets, minor prophets, religious poetry, and a few others.

Also, if you would like to do further study on this, it would certainly be worth your time to delve into the differences between the Christian and Jewish categorization. Yes, this is a Christian book, but we must remember that our Jewish brothers and sisters are maintaining the tradition from which Christ was born. Christians must never abandon a Jewish understanding of the Old Testament—otherwise we lose so much clarity and structure in properly understanding the whole of scripture.

As you progress through this book, an overview of each genre will precede the books contained therein. In addition, if you choose to use this as a tool alongside your personal Bible study, it would be worth reading the genre's overview prior to reading the book you're working through.

May God bless you and keep you.

CHAPTER 6

Law

(Encouragement to serve God based upon evidence)

Everything worthwhile in life must be formed upon a solid foundation. This is true of relationships, buildings, careers, education, skill sets, etc.—and, yes, even religious belief. Providing this solid foundation for religious belief is where the Old Testament genre we call "Law" steps up and shines with purpose. It does so by delineating a strong set of nonnegotiable teachings regarding:

1. The truth about God
2. The truth about humanity
3. His expectations
4. How we are to interact with Him
5. How we are to interact with one another

The five books contained in the Law are the foundation of all biblical understanding.

Read that sentence again.

Now read it again.

Since they serve as the foundation of all other biblical revelation, it is only natural to find these books at the beginning of the Bible. As we look to read, study, and apply the five books of Genesis, Exodus, Leviticus, Numbers and Deuteronomy, let us never forget *these five books, comprised as a single unit, serve as the sole footing upon which our entire faith is built.* This is critical to understand.

In the original Hebrew language, these five books are known as Torah (תּוֹרָה) and to this day they are still referenced as such by the Jewish community and many Christians worldwide. While Torah literally means "teaching," the most familiar meaning of the word is "the five books of Moses."[10] They are labeled this because Moses is traditionally considered the author or at least the formal composer.

The Greek name for Torah is Pentateuch. It's debated among scholars as to when this name was first used, but we know that "the Rabbinic writers adopted the expression 'the five-fifths of the law' or simply 'the five-fifths' to denote the five books of the Pentateuch."[11]

To properly understand and implement the Law into common everyday life, contemporary Christians must follow the blueprint set before them by the original recipients of Torah. So, who were these original recipients and what did the Torah mean to them? The Torah "was originally meant to encourage ancient Israelites to believe and trust in God because of His faithful relationship with their ancestors."[12] The people of Israel were being encouraged through the Law to stay true to God. They were given good reason to do so: He was faithful to their ancestors, which was to serve as a solid indicator that He would be faithful to them as well!

Just like our lives, the lives of the original audience was filled with constant ebb and flow. They had good days, and they had bad days. They celebrated life, and they mourned death. And just as you and I are tempted daily to become self-centered sinful creatures, so too were the ancient Israelites. The Israelite nation needed to be reminded of all the wonderful truths about their God, and the Torah served as this reminder.

These wonderful truths about God were given to the original recipients, as well as to you and me, using some of the best storytelling ever written.

---

[10] Jacob Neusner, *The Emergence of Judaism* (Louisville: Westminster John Knox Press, 2004), 57.

[11] Anthony Maas, *Pentateuch*, in *The Catholic Encyclopedia*. Vol. 11. (New York: Robert Appleton Company, 1911. 24 Apr. 2021 <http://www.newadvent.org/cathen/11646c.htm>.

[12] Bill T. Arnold and Bryan E. Beyer, *Encountering Biblical Studies, Encountering the Old Testament,* ed. Eugene H. Merrill (Grand Rapids, MI: Baker Book House, 1999), 64.

Within the Law we find so many great stories told in such beautifully written fashion that even the unbeliever can appreciate the prowess of the writer. However, the Torah is not just a conglomeration of *great* stories; it's also a conglomeration of *true* stories. True stories that teach us about God, His ways, and our responsibility to Him. Check out just a few of the bigger highlights below:

Adam and Eve (Genesis 1–4)—God creates ... we destroy ... God rebuilds.

Noah (Genesis 5–9)—The Lord is faithful ... to the faithful.

The Tower of Babel (Genesis 11)—The pride of man cannot stand against God.

Abraham (Genesis 12–25)—God can use a pagan to save the world.

Joseph (Genesis 37–50)—Even in a pit ... even in a prison ... we are being molded for purpose.

Moses (Exodus, Leviticus, Numbers, and Deuteronomy)—God always has a plan of deliverance.

The Passover (Exodus 12)—Those covered by the blood will be passed over when God's justice is served.

The Ten Commandments (Exodus 20, Deuteronomy 5)—God has given us a moral code.

The sacrificial system (Leviticus)—The cost of sin is death.

The priesthood (Leviticus)—God works among His people.

Many more ...

Scholars are divided on whether the Torah was meant to be taken literally. However, from our perspective, we are to take the stories literally *and* apply them literally into our lives, as a general rule. Grappling with more specific and concrete application will be handled later as each of the five books are addressed individually. However, please remember, as you deal with each book, they were intended to be read as a single unit. Please allow your interpretation of each book to tie back into and support the Big Idea of the whole genre that *God is encouraging you and I through the Law to stay true to Him.* We're given good reason and evidence to do so in that He was faithful to our ancestors, which means He will be faithful to us as well.

The Concept of Covenant

The foundation upon which God demonstrated His faithfulness in Torah was demonstrated by making covenants with His people. One such covenant that serves as a prime example is the one between Him and Abram. In Genesis 15 God reached out to Abram and "cut a covenant" with him that changed all human history. The story goes something like this.

In Genesis 15, Abram expressed concern to God that he had no child as an heir. In response, God "cut a covenant" with Abram that his descendants would be as numerous as the stars. The Bible then states: "Abram believed the Lord, and he credited it to him as righteousness" (Genesis 15:6 NIV). Abram is then reminded that God was guiding his life as the scripture states: "He also said to him, 'I am the Lord, who brought you out of Ur of the Chaldeans to give you this land to take possession of it.' But Abram said, 'O Sovereign Lord, how can I know that I will gain possession of it?'"

At this point, God instructed Abram to do something so extraordinarily significant—yet we contemporary folks completely miss it unless we're familiar with ancient contractual agreements. God instructed Abram to fetch a heifer, a goat, a ram, a dove, and a young pigeon. He then instructed Abram to cut the animals in half (not the birds) and arrange the halves opposite one other, creating a hallway of sorts through which God would pass. Most of us today have no idea of the significance of what took place, but Abram knew exactly what God was doing! "The act of dividing the animals and walking through the parts was apparently an ancient form of contractual agreement."[13]

The type of treaty God was making with Abram most closely resembles a "suzerainty treaty" and was common throughout the ancient Near East. God was essentially sealing the deal between Him and Abram with blood. This type of treaty required both parties to walk down the hallway of the sacrificed animals as they stated the terms of the agreement. In the ancient world, the more powerful party, known as the "suzerain" would state the terms of the agreement with a series of if/then statements directed at the

---

[13] John H. Sailhamer, "Genesis," In *The Expositor's Bible Commentary, vol. 2,* Frank E. Gaebelein, ed. (Grand Rapids, MI: Zondervan, 1979), 130.

weaker party, known as the vassal. Basically, "*If* you keep your terms, *then* I will protect you and make you succeed, but *if* you do not keep your terms, *then* I will end you." This is exactly the deal cut with Abram, and it is the basis of salvation as found in all scripture.

If we follow God, *then* He will bless us.

If we turn away from Him, *then* curses will follow.

This may seem a bit offensive to our twenty-first century audience, but it is straight from the Torah, straight from the Law, straight from God's Word. The covenant God made with us through Abraham is based upon an if/then statement. Like it or not, it is what it is.

So with such dire consequences to the vassal upon breaking their contract, they needed to know that the suzerain was also committed to the death. To demonstrate their commitment, the suzerain would also walk down the hallway of death and call the same thing upon himself if he broke his side of the treaty. As one scholar states: "there seems to be a fairly consistent interpretation of the act as a kind of self-imprecation, as though the participants in the treaty would say, 'If I break the treaty may this happen to me.'"[14]

OK, pause … In case you're wondering if you read this correctly, yes, God was welcoming death upon himself if he broke the covenant with Abram! This may sound almost heretical to our twenty-first century ears, but that's simply what was taking place between God and Abram. Knowing this is critical as we make the most futile attempt at grasping God's love for us. Though we can never truly grasp His love, we need to understand that He was and is willing to die … God knew Abram needed reassurance to remain faithful to Him. So … He very literally put Himself on death row as insurance to Abram and to you and me!

This story is indescribably pivotal in understanding Torah, the Bible, and God's unending love for us! Essentially, if God is *alive*, He hasn't stopped loving us. While this is truly impossible for our tiny little human brains and hearts to fully grasp, it is still mind-blowing!

Be obedient, be blessed.

Now the time has come to narrow our focus of Torah by looking at the details of each of the five books contained therein. As we do this, we will look at the following categories of each book: Big Idea, author,

---

[14] J. A. Thompson, *The Ancient Near Eastern Treaties and the Old Testament* (London: Tyndale Press, 1964), 25.

original recipients, date of writing, historical setting/timeline of events, main characters, purpose, key scripture(s) and theme(s), and contemporary application. The purpose of this is to provide a very brief and non-exhaustive introduction to each book. Hopefully, this will assist you in continuing your study as you continue to dive deeper beyond that which is covered here.

Genesis

Big Idea
The Creator of the cosmos controls the chaos.

Author
Moses. Theologians debate Moses's authorship of Genesis and the whole Torah, but traditionally he has been credited as the author. For our purposes we'll stick with Moses.

Original Recipients
Ancient Israel was the original recipient of this work.

Date of Writing
Moses wrote Genesis (and the whole Torah) sometime shortly after the Exodus of 1446 BCE. See "Exodus: Historical Setting/Timeline of Events" for an analysis/documentation on the date of the Exodus.

Historical Setting/Timeline of Events
Genesis takes us from the creation through the death of Joseph in 1805 BCE.[15]

Main Characters
God (Timeless), Adam and Eve (date unknown), Noah (Date unknown), Abraham (2166–1991 BC), Isaac (2066–1886 BC), Jacob (2006–1859 BC), Joseph (1915–1805 BC)[16]

Purpose
Genesis is a book that is naturally divided into two parts. Genesis 1–11 sets the stage for the remainder of the Pentateuch and the entire Bible by introducing God, His creation, and the fallen nature of humankind. While there are stories in these first eleven chapters dealing with individual people

---

[15] John H. Walton, *Chronological and Background Charts of the Old Testament* (Grand Rapids, MI: Zondervan, 1994), 15. (John Walton follows the Masoretic Text for these dates).

[16] Ibid.

and families, this section can be thought of more so as a general description of the world's scene. The second part takes a different turn and chapters 12–50 is where we see the grace, mercy, and love of God as He reveals the beginnings of His plan to restore us from the fall. God does this by leaving the mile high perspective of chapters 1–11 and zooms in on one family—the lineage of Abraham.

So, in essence, the first eleven chapters open the Bible with the very serious problem of the fall and the last thirty-nine chapters present the solution. Adam and Eve messed it up, but God would save His creation through using the lineage of Abraham that would ultimately bring about Jesus Christ.

Key Scripture(s) and Theme(s)

As with all books of the Bible, we could reference a handful of scriptures to give us a clear idea of the main thrust of the book. However, for our purposes, we will focus on one verse. In this one verse God speaks to Abraham and says: "I will establish my covenant as an everlasting covenant between me and you and your descendants after you for the generations to come, to be your God and the God of your descendants after you" (Genesis 17:7).

This key verse helps us grasp the three main themes of Genesis.

1. The loving nature of God. God displayed His loving nature by first creating everything and identifying it as "good" (Genesis 1:4, 10, 12, 18, 21, 25, 31). However, soon thereafter, humankind ruined it so God again displayed His loving nature by reaching out to Abraham (Genesis 12) to make a covenant that would last forever. It is vital to know that this covenant, and only this covenant, is the natural spring from which the great river of His salvation begins.

Many folks look at the Old Testament and see a God whose hands are always in the ready position to throw violent blows of harsh, brutal, and unmerciful judgment at humanity. This could not be any further from the truth! On the contrary, God has always been a loving, compassionate Good

Shepherd, and this is revealed to us in the book of Genesis. It is here that He reaches out to begin the process of saving humanity.

As a matter of fact, long before the covenant with Abraham, God began to institute His plan of salvation. We see the fall take place in Genesis 3:1–7 concluding with Adam and Eve sewing fig leaves together to cover themselves as they realized they were naked. The realization that they were naked is simply symbolic for the reality that they no longer contained their innocence—they had decided to go against the instruction of our perfect Creator. At this point, God *immediately* began his plan of salvation by seeking them out, finding them, and replacing their half-hazard leaves with the skins of animals (Genesis 3:21).

Now how in the world is this the beginning of His loving plan of salvation? Think about it this way:

a. Fig leaves would have to be continually replaced. This was indicative of the temporary nature of the human solution.
b. In contrast to Adam and Eve's temporary solution, God's solution was permanent. He clothed them with the leather hide of animals.

Have you ever seen a skinless cow in the field? No. Anytime you remove the skin from a creature, it dies. So what we see here is God removing the life from precious creatures that He had previously breathed it into. Sound familiar? This taking of life was the first glance or foreshadowing we see in scripture of God's ultimate plan to permanently rid us of our fallen nature through the taking of Christ's life. What an amazing act of love! What an amazing display of the loving nature of our God!

2. The fallen nature Of humanity. It is true that humans can be and are very good people. We act in kindness, generosity, faithfulness, and love daily worldwide. However, Genesis 3 firmly establishes the concrete truth that when left to our own devices, we are very fallen and full of rot. Many critics of Christianity poke fun by saying, "Why would God make a garden with poison fruit and a talking reptile?" And, honestly, when it's stated like that, it sounds just as silly and untrue as so many other creation stories scattered throughout human civilizations. However, the whole point of

the story of the fall is very simple: God wanted to share true love between himself and His creation. To do this, He had to give His creation free will—the ability to choose right from wrong. "Right" is to be understood as obedience, and "wrong" is to be understood as disobedience. Well, we humans decided to disobey, making us imperfect. That created a dilemma in that God is perfect and humans are not. Much like oil and water cannot mix, so too, perfection and imperfection cannot mix, so we are left with a separation between us and God. Human nature truly is fallen.

3. The instituting of God's plan to restore broken humanity.

God's plan to restore us ultimately culminates in the New Testament with the death and resurrection of Jesus Christ. But how in the world are we supposed to understand how the death of one person can result in the life of all others? This is where God's progressive revelation steps in and begins to slowly reveal to us over the centuries exactly how that works. The New Testament tells us in Galatians 4:4 that "when the right time came, God sent his Son …" (New Living Translation). There are several reasons why the "right time" wasn't much earlier, but the crux of it rests in this idea of God's progressive revelation.

Think of it this way: if God had become flesh in Jesus Christ immediately after the fall of Genesis 3, we humans would have had no idea of what was going on. The question would have probably been posed something like: How can blood being shed for me in the physical realm save me from the spiritual realm? It just would not have made sense, and God knew this. So, being the omniscient Creator He is, God took the hand of humanity and slowly began to lead them down His path that slowly revealed to us one slow step at a time His action plan for eternal success. This action plan culminates in Jesus Christ but begins with the covenant He made with Abraham.

Contemporary Application

First and foremost, the book of Genesis lays the foundation for all we know about God. In contemporary times, we have the Bible in its completed and final form. However, the original recipients of Genesis knew nothing that we so unknowingly take for granted. What we know about God as described in the book of Genesis is that He is:

a. a very creative being. He created all things (Genesis 1–2).
b. a very loving being. Even while holding us accountable for our sin, He searches us out (Genesis 3:8–21).
c. a very merciful and gracious being. After God had cursed (held accountable) the serpent, the woman, and the man (Genesis 3:14–19), He furnished the greatest form of mercy and grace imaginable by banishing us from the garden. Many people see this as an extension of the curses brought upon us, but it was actually the greatest blessing He could have bestowed. Scripture tells us that if we had stayed in the garden and eaten from the tree of life, we would have lived forever in our sin (Genesis 3:22–24). What a horrible thing!

The second application from Genesis is that we should all walk in humility. Yes, God made us "good," but we, by our own choice, became rotten at our very core. It's quite an intriguing study to look at theologians' pre-World War era and post-World War era views on the nature of humanity. Prior to the great wars of the 1900s, many scholars had decided that we humans were basically good. However, the great wars truly shook the world, causing the pendulum to swing back the other direction to better align with scripture. Certainly, we are good in so many ways, but our very nature itself is violent, treacherous, selfish, arrogant, cruel, and bent on doing things our way. Thank God for His salvation!

The last and final main application that we draw from Genesis is short and simple: God has a plan for each of us to be saved from ourselves. Furthermore, we know from Genesis that God is willing to do whatever it takes to save us—He even went so far as to spill blood and kill precious creatures to cover us, symbolizing and foretelling the blood that would eventually be spilled by Jesus Christ. God will stop at absolutely nothing to save us, and this is why we can say with wholehearted security that *the Creator of the cosmos controls the chaos!*

Exodus

Big Idea

The Lord saves the slaves.

Author

Moses. See "Author" on Genesis for more information.

Original Recipients

Ancient Israel.

Date of Writing

Sometime shortly after the Exodus of 1446 BCE. See discussion below on the date of the Exodus.

Historical Setting/Timeline of Events

Exodus tells the story of God rescuing His people from Egyptian slavery (1:1–12:36), guiding them through the desert (12:37–18:27), and the giving of the law and tabernacle at Mount Sinai (19–40). All these events took place in 1446 BCE, beginning with the Exodus.

Much debate has arisen regarding the date of the Exodus, but the biblical record itself demands it took place in the fifteenth century BCE. According to 1 Kings 6:1, it began either 1446 BCE or 1406 BCE.[17][18]. It is generally agreed upon that the 1446 BCE date is more accurate as

---

[17] For a detailed analysis see Paul J. Ray Jr., "The Duration of the Israelite Sojourn in Egypt," Bible and Spade 17 (2004): 33–44. The 1446 BCE date is backed by the Masoretic Text (the Hebrew text from which most Bibles are translated) and the 1406 date is supported by the Septuagint (third century AD Greek translation of the Hebrew text). Additionally, Paul's speech in Acts 13:17–21 gives us a date of 1536 BCE. All three dates are supported by our current understanding of the biblical texts. Whichever date you go with, the theology doesn't change, but you are encouraged to study it for yourself and decide.

[18] Edwin R. Thiele, *The Mysterious Numbers of the Hebrew Kings* (Grand Rapids, MI: Eerdmans, 1965), 51–53.

it is based on the Masoretic Text versus the Septuagint.[19] However, for a good comparison/contrast between the fifteenth and thirteenth century perspectives, please note John H. Walton's *Chronological and Background Charts of the Old Testament*.[20]

Main Characters

Moses, Pharaoh, Israelite nation.

Purpose

Exodus, as a part of the Torah, is a continuation of the Genesis narrative. It was written to provide a historical record of God's people from the time of Egyptian slavery until they escaped and reached Mount Sinai in the desert. Additionally, it provides a record of how serious God is about continuing His covenant with humanity to provide a rescue from sin. It focuses on providing details of the deliverance from slavery, the giving of the Ten Commandments, as well as providing details for the building of the tabernacle.

Key Scripture(s) and Theme(s)

"And when the Israelites saw the mighty hand of the Lord displayed against the Egyptians, the people feared the Lord and put their trust in Him and in Moses His servant" Exodus 14:31.

Contemporary Application

1. Simply put: *God rescues us.* The Exodus out of Egypt is referenced several times throughout the Bible as a reminder of how God rescues His people. Our God is a rescuing God that will never give up on us. Even the same people that walked out of Egypt as free turned their backs on God in the book of Exodus, but God didn't give up on them. This provides us with incredible hope to

---

[19] For more detail see Peter J. Gentry, "The Septuagint and the Text of the Old Testament," BBR 16 (2006): 193–218. Also, Karen H. Jobes, "When God Spoke Greek: The Place of the Greek Bible in Evangelical Scholarship," BBR 16 (2006): 219–36.

[20] John H. Walton, *Chronological and Background Charts of the Old Testament* (Grand Rapids, MI: Zondervan, 1994), 102–3.

know that regardless of how far we are into our own sin, God will always be there to provide rescue.

2. God desires relationship. After the Israelites were freed from slavery, God led them through the desert to the foot of Mount Sinai where He gave all sorts of laws including the Ten Commandments. He then followed them up with directions on how to build a portable temple called the tabernacle. All the laws and the tabernacle were given to provide proper relationship between us and God.

It did this in two ways. First, the Ten Commandments and all other laws given at the time are very similar to rules we may have in our own contemporary homes. For example, with our children we set up rules that provide a context for the family relationship to thrive. The same is true with God. First, He has set up His own set of "house rules" that clearly outline how we are to relate to Him and His people (i.e., have no other gods before me, keep the sabbath holy, don't lie, don't murder, etc.) Relationships simply cannot last unless clear guidelines are given as to how that relationship is to work. Thank God that He provided them for us! Second, the tabernacle represents God's presence—it's where He came down to dwell among His people. God surely desires to dwell among His people today, and that includes you as an individual. First Corinthians 3:16 tells us: "Don't you know that you yourselves are God's temple and that God's Spirit dwells in your midst." We are the temple of the Lord, and God desires to embrace relationship with us!

And these two points of application from the book of Exodus establish the Big Idea that *the Lord saves the slaves!*

Leviticus

Big Idea
Be holy for I am holy.

Author
Moses. Theologians have highly debated Moses's authorship in recent scholarship, but traditionally Moses has been credited as being the author.

Original Recipients
Much of the book was written to the Levites who were one of the twelve tribes of Israel. However, Leviticus 1:2 tells of how God told Moses to "speak to the Israelites ..." so we know it was originally meant for *all* of God's ancient people.

Date of Writing
Leviticus was written within one year of the Exodus of 1446 BCE—most likely within the last few months of that year before the Israelites left Mount Sinai. As discussed earlier under "Exodus: Historical Setting/ Timeline of Events," two main dates are proposed by theologians for the Exodus. The date you choose will not affect the theology or application.

Historical Setting/Timeline of Events
The children of Israel were at the foot of Mount Sinai and had already received the Ten Commandments as well as many other laws. They had already completed the building of the tabernacle and were probably preparing to exit the foot of Mount Sinai.

Main Characters
God, Moses, Levites, Israelites

Purpose
Leviticus was written to communicate to the Israelites that God is unexplainably holy and they, therefore, were to strive for holiness as well. To make this point, God provided clear instructions to the Levites on how He was to be worshipped. The sacrificial system and laws were all given to make their worship holy and acceptable to the One and Only Holy God.

"Whereas Exodus ended by emphasizing *where* to worship God (i.e., the tabernacle), Leviticus deals with *how* to worship Him."[21]

Key Scripture(s) and Theme(s)

"The Lord said to Moses, 'Speak to the entire assembly of Israel and say to them: 'Be holy because I, the Lord your God, am holy'" (Leviticus 19:1–2).

Holiness is the central theme of Leviticus as it clearly outlines how God is to be viewed, respected, and addressed.

Contemporary Application

1. God Is holy. God is not an old, white-bearded man seated on a cloud aloof to reality. He is also not a mean, fiery God perched on that same cloud waiting to fling lightning bolts at us. On the contrary, God is indescribably sacred, holy, and worthy of much more respect than we humans can give. While it may be appropriate to sometimes describe God as our friend, it tends to portray a casual, nonchalant relationship with Him. In contrast, we are reminded in Leviticus that we *cannot* approach God on our terms. He is to be approached with extreme humility and awe.

Think of it this way—if you were to meet the president of the United States or the queen of England, would you march in, plop yourself down, and just begin to give an earful? Absolutely not! You would walk in with a reverent posture and respectfully wait to be addressed. Now I'm not comparing a human with God, but we should certainly approach the throne of Grace with the understanding that God holds all in His hands and *he* is the one that dictates how we interact with Him. It is never our way with God—it is always His way. Love it or hate it, agree or disagree, but that's just the way it is, period.

Sadly, many of the recent generations have lost this concept. Back in the early 2000s, a T-shirt circulated widely among youth groups that stated: "God is my homeboy." I was a youth pastor back then, and I

---

[21] Bill T. Arnold and Bryan E. Beyer, *Encountering Biblical Studies, Encountering the Old Testament*, ed. Eugene H. Merrill (Grand Rapids, MI: Baker Book House, 1999), 119.

kindly guided the youth under our care to think twice about wearing it. Friends, God is not our "homeboy" or our "hang out buddy." God is the Holy Creator of the cosmos, and that should stir up something within us that desires to address Him on His terms! Either way, even if we think we have a "special agreement" of some sort with God, we are wrong. Without addressing Him on His terms, we simply do not have the ability to enter His presence. Leviticus teaches us this.

2. Because God is holy, we are to be holy. This all falls back on God's desire to be in relation with us. God is holy, cannot become unholy, and cannot "mix" with unholiness. Therefore, for us to have relationship with Him, we must become holy. This is really the whole problem with our sin—and it is exactly why God instituted the Old Testament system that foretold and ushered in the work of Jesus Christ. "Our holiness is derived from Him, as we live in fellowship with Him and learn to obey His will with the help of His Holy Spirit."[22]

To better help us drive this point deep into our hearts, we must look at the definition of the word *holy* and how it related to the Levites. The word *holy* means "set apart." God was set apart from all things imperfect—He had to distance Himself from all things imperfect. By definition, if perfection (God) mixed with imperfection (us) either God would be made imperfect, or we would be made perfect. Obviously, God will always be perfect, so how do we as imperfect creatures mix into Perfection and become perfect ourselves? Well, it starts right here in the books of Moses with God giving the Law and instituting the sacrificial system. It is here that the Levites were "set apart" from the rest of Israel to carry out the tabernacle duties. It's here in the books of Moses (first five books of the Bible) that God begins the centuries-long process of preparing the minds of His people for the Messiah. And God prepared the minds of the people for this death of Jesus through the continual sacrifices made by the holy priesthood. Leviticus teaches us this.

And just as the Levites were set apart to ensure proper relationship and worship, we too have been set apart from defilement to ensure proper worship takes place inside us. And this is the meaning of *be holy for I am holy.*

---

[22] Ibid., 125.

Numbers

Big Idea

God demonstrates His dedication by disciplining disobedience

Author

Moses.

Original Recipients

Ancient Israel.

Date of Writing

Moses most likely wrote Numbers as the events were taking place during the forty years of wandering in the desert and/or immediately following this period just before his death around 1406 BCE.

Historical Setting/Timeline of Events

Numbers picks up where Leviticus leaves off. Leviticus describes events that took place at Mount Sinai during the first year of Israelite freedom from Egyptian slavery. Numbers picks up the narrative at this point and provides a chronology we can separate into three parts based on their changes in geographical location:

1. Numbers 1:1–10:10 details God giving Israel instructions and preparations for the journey from Mount Sinai to the promised land.
2. Numbers 10:11–20:21 describes events that took place during the nearly forty years the Israelites wandered in the desert.
3. Numbers 20:22–36:13 describes their time spent on the plains of Moab preparing to enter the promised land.

Main Characters

God, Moses, Disobedient Israel

Purpose

Though Numbers records roughly forty years of Israel's history, this is not the purpose. The real purpose is twofold.

1. "Numbers is not a history of Israel, but an essay about the consequences of disobedience."[23] From the time they began preparations to leave Mount Sinai, the people displayed a rebellious heart. Though the people began their outcries of disbelief and disobedience toward God in 11:1, chapters 13 and 14 record Israel's ultimate failure to trust God by refusing to enter the Promised Land. Chapter 13 tells of the famous story of twelve spies sent to spy out the land. Of the twelve only two, Joshua and Caleb, brought back a positive report. The other ten claimed, "We can't attack those people; they are stronger than we are" (Numbers 13:31 NIV). The people responded in chapter 14 with the ultimate slap in God's face: "If only we had died in Egypt … wouldn't it be better if we go back to Egypt!?" (Numbers 14:2–3 NIV).

God's initial response was to destroy them, but Moses pleaded for forgiveness in their behalf resulting in a lesser punishment of banning every person twenty years or older from entering the Promised Land. This resulted in the forty years of desert wandering. It's interesting to note that the starting point and ending point of their forty years of wandering was actually only about a forty-day journey. In essence, their disobedience turned a forty-day journey into a forty-year journey!

2. Despite Israel's disobedience, God displayed mercy by remaining faithful to the covenant He made with Abraham. Regardless of Israel's unfaithfulness, God remained faithful, and He demonstrated this by raising the next generation to take the land—to continue God's historical work of providing salvation to His people that would eventually culminate in Jesus Christ.

Key Scripture(s) and Theme(s)

"Not one of those who saw my glory and the signs I performed in Egypt and in the wilderness but who disobeyed me and tested me ten time—not one of them will ever see the land I promised on oath to their ancestors. No one who has treated me with contempt will ever see it. But because my servant Caleb has a different spirit and followed me wholeheartedly, I

---

[23] Ibid., 134.

will bring him into the land he went to, and his descendants will inherit it" (Numbers 14:22–24).

Contemporary Application

Ronald B. Allen sums up Numbers quite well and provides a solid springboard for some intense application:

Those whom God had redeemed from slavery in Egypt and to whom He had displayed His grace at Mount Sinai responded with indifference, ingratitude, and repeated acts of rebellion. The community of the redeemed was punished by the Lord by being forbidden to enter the Promised Land. They were made to live out their lives in the Desert of Sinai; only their children would enjoy the promise that was originally to be theirs.[24]

The cold, hard truth is that when we disobey God, there are real and severe consequences. However, we would be wise to follow in the steps of the generation following the Exodus generation and choose to trust and obey regardless of what we think about His direction. Afterall, who is better at discerning what is best for us: the all-knowing Creator of the cosmos or us little tiny humans?

We should also learn from Numbers that while God's plan will always succeed, we are called to fully buy into His will and wholeheartedly engage ourselves with the flow of His will. So I ask myself the question: Am I fully engaged in the mission God has for me and my family? If not, where do I need to realign?

Despite the continual rebellion of God's people in Numbers, the mercy of God is also extended in that the following generation was raised to take their place and become the generation to enter and take the Promised Land. God's plan prevailed in biblical times, and it will also prevail in contemporary times. Regardless of our sin, His ultimate plan of salvation will always continue marching forward throughout all time and all nations. This is why we can conclude from Numbers that *God demonstrates His dedication by discipling disobedience* among us as His children.

So the final question is this: Are you going to rebel and receive His discipline, or are you going to take the Promised Land? Only you can answer that.

---

[24] Ronald B. Allen, "Numbers," In *The Expositor's Bible Commentary*, vol. 2, ed. Frank E. Gaebelein (Grand Rapids, MI: Zondervan, 1979), 662.

Deuteronomy

Big Idea

God is faithful to every generation, and every generation is called to be faithful to Him.

Author

Though tradition and most conservative theologians claim Moses wrote Deuteronomy, there has recently been debate among theologians. Several contemporary theologians claim that Deuteronomy, along with Joshua, Judges, the Samuels, and the Kings (known as the Former Prophets in the Hebrew Bible) were written as a single literary work we now call Deuteronomistic History (DH). The theory claims that an unknown author wrote sometime after the Babylonians conquered Judah in 586 BCE and was reflecting on the loss of the kingdom.[25] Under this perspective is the view that portions of these books were probably written by other people but were later compiled in the form we now have today by this "Deuteronomic" author.

We are going to stick with the more traditional and conservative perspective that Moses wrote Deuteronomy. However, regardless of who is correct, we can rest assure that we're still reading God's Word, and it still holds significant meaning for us today.

Original Recipients

Ancient Israel.

Date of Writing

Deuteronomy was written just prior to the death of Moses around 1406 BCE. The Israelites were preparing the take the Promised Land at this time.

---

[25] Gary N. Knoppers and Jonathan S. Greer. *Deuteronomistic History*. Oxford Bibliography Online: Biblical Studies. Ed. C. Matthews; New York: Oxford University Press. 2010.

Historical Setting/Timeline of Events

The Exodus generation had just wandered in the desert for forty years due to their disobedience, and the last of them had died. Deuteronomy picks up where Numbers left off in the plains of Moab. Here the people are ready to cross the Jordan River and take the Promised Land.

Main Characters

God, Moses, the generation of Israelites that would conquer the Promised Land.

Purpose

The word *Deuteronomy* means "second law" which gives us great insight into the book's purpose. This new generation of Israelites had not witnessed the great miracles of the Exodus. They needed a reminder that God was with them if they remained faithful to Him. So, in Deuteronomy, God *reestablishes* His covenant with them, a second giving of the law.

This book contains three speeches from Moses where he encourages the people to remain faithful to God. Moses desires to prepare the new generation for the Promised Land by revisiting and reminding them of the miracles God had performed in the previous generation.

Speech 1 is found in 1:1–4:43 and recaps God's provision from the covenant at Mount Sinai to where they were in that moment on the plains of Moab.

Speech 2, found in 4:44–26:19, served as a reminder of the laws given in Exodus 20–23. This was a new generation in a different set of circumstances, so they needed to understand how to apply the Ten Commandments into their specific situation.

Speech 3 is found in 27:1–31:30. Here we find Moses stating that either curses or blessings would fall upon them depending upon their response to God's direction. He also formally confirms Joshua as his successor.

The book closes with the "Song of Moses" (chapter 32), the "Blessing of Moses" (chapter 33), and the death and burial of Moses (chapter 34).

Key Scripture(s) and Theme(s)

"These are the commands, decrees and laws the Lord your God directed me to teach you to observe in the land that you are crossing the Jordan to possess, so that you, your children and their children after them may fear the Lord your God as long as you live by keeping all His decrees and commands that I give you, and so that you may enjoy long life. Hear, Israel, and be careful to obey so that it may go well with you and that you may increase greatly in a land flowing with milk and honey, just as the Lord, the God of your ancestors, promised you. Hear, O Israel: The Lord our God, the Lord is one. Love the Lord your God with all your heart and with all your soul and with all your strength. These commandments that I give you today are to be on your hearts. Impress them on your children. Talk about them when you sit at home and when you walk along the road, when you lie down and when you get up. Tie them as symbols on your hands and bind them on your foreheads. Write them on the doorframes of your houses and on your gates" (Deuteronomy 6:1–9).

Contemporary Application

The most significant application we can pull from Deuteronomy is found in Moses's second speech, found in 27:1–31:30. Here we learn that, just as we see in other books of the Torah, it is our job to either align ourselves with God and receive His blessings or live life on our own terms and bring upon ourselves curses. Our contemporary society is the epitome of living life based upon our own will instead of that of God's will. Sadly, this mentality has crept into the church, and we would be wise to distance ourselves from it. God is not a negotiator. It's either His way or no way. Very simply, we come to God on His terms, or we are cast from His presence. There is no compromise.

On a more positive note, Deuteronomy encourages us to remember who God is and what He has done for us so that we will choose to follow Him and dwell in His presence and blessings. Each generation must have God's covenant inscribed upon their hearts as well as given an understanding and solid application of His Word into their circumstances. Our key scripture from Deuteronomy 6, known in the Jewish community as the Shema, is one of the first scriptures young Jewish boys memorize because of its significance in our lives. We are to surround ourselves with God's Word, His Will, and His Way if we are to reap the reward of being His harvest.

Stick with God and enjoy a fruitful life full of blessing! This doesn't mean we'll have a perfect earthly life, but it does mean we'll have a perfect eternity! Stay the course! Remember, *God is faithful to every generation, and every generation is called to be faithful to Him.*

CHAPTER 7

Historical Books

Joshua, Judges, Ruth, 1 and 2 Samuel, 1 and 2 Kings, 1 and 2 Chronicles, Ezra, Nehemiah, and Esther make up the Old Testament historical books. In these books one will find a very rich, colorful, dark, vibrant, haunting, and beautiful ancient world. For this reason, "readers with historical interests will naturally gravitate to the OT historical narratives for information about life in ancient Israel and the ancient Near East."[26]

As we begin to peer into the world of the ancient Near East through the lens of these books, it is almost impossible to escape the ever-changing horizon of thick plot twists, heroic characters, incredible feats, and glorious triumphs. And yet we also see painted very clearly the other side of humanity as these books make no effort to tone down the reality of its many blood-bathed battles, treacherous regrets, deceitful coverups, and the proliferation of immorality on the world's scene among God's people.

Chronologically, the historical books begin about 1405 BC, after the death of Moses, and tell the story of a people filled with the same back-and-forth experience that contemporary Christians sometimes seem to think are unique to only their day. All in all, the historical books continue telling the story of a very Good God as He marches His plan of salvation through human history, regardless of the obstacles that humans continually prop up in His path.

Mary Fairchild, in her article titled "Historical Books," provides a solid

---

[26] David M. Howard Jr. *An Introduction To The Old Testament Historical Books.* (Chicago: Moody Press, 1993), 23.

beginning point for proper interpretation and application as she sums up this genre quite well:

> After Joshua, the history books take us through Israel's ups and downs under Judges, its transition to kingship, the division of the nation, and its life as two rival kingdoms (Israel and Judah), the moral decline and exile of both kingdoms, the period of captivity, and finally, the nation's return from exile. The historical books cover almost an entire millennium of Israel's history. As we read these pages of the Bible, we relive incredible stories and meet fascinating leaders, prophets, heroes, and villains. Through their real-life adventures, some of failure and some of victory, we identify personally with these characters and learn valuable lessons from their lives.[27]

With Fairchild's assessment in mind, we will look at a twofold purpose for this genre (not in order of importance).

1. **To provide a historical context within which to interpret biblical events**

The first purpose was to provide a historical context within which the ancient Israelite events could be interpreted. This is to be clearly understood as different than providing a historical record. The original audience was very familiar with their history and so the intent of the historical books was *not* to be their official history. As Bill T. Arnold states in his contribution to the *NIV Application Commentary*:

> Today's readers sometimes forget the Bible's "historical books" were not meant to present a history of Israel and that we as Christians are not nurtured primarily by a study of history in and of itself … we should remember their real nature as sermonic tracts. They invite us to follow the historical acts of God in early Israel. They

---

[27] Mary Fairchild, "Historical Books." Learn Religions, Aug. 25, 2020, learnreligions. com/historical-books-of-the-bible-700269.

illustrate indirectly or subtly truths explained more directly elsewhere in Scripture.[28]

In essence, without the historical books, the events during this time would be of no real significance, just simply the stories of nations and people like any other secular history. However, this Old Testament genre teaches us *how we are to interpret the historical events contained therein.* They provide a lens through which we look at these events as not just mere historical human affairs but more so as the *spiritual journey, successes, and failures of God's people as He fulfills His plan in their lives.*

Another way of stating this is to say the historical books give theological or spiritual meaning to the chronological history of Israel. A notable example of this is to look at the many battles God's people fought in the historical books. As the people of God, it was simply understood that victory was expected, yet they lost several battles. How does this make sense? It's likely that they thought to themselves, *We are God's chosen people, and yet we just lost this battle to a much lesser army! This is ridiculous!* And, yes, ridiculous it was! Yet, there was always a spiritual reason for each physical loss.

The classic example of this is found in Joshua 7. The Israelites had just won a great battle against Jericho and turned their attention to a much feebler city called Ai and lost to them! Upon being defeated by Ai, it was quickly revealed to the Israelites that sin was in the camp. A man named Achan had taken some of the plunder from the victory over Jericho, which was in clear disobedience to God. So, until they purged this sin, God was not with them in battle. Without the historical books we would not have this spiritual explanation for the loss. In the historical books, we are given a historical context within which to find solid interpretation.

With this genre covering approximately one thousand years of history, we cannot be surprised to find other forms of biblical genres falling within the timeline of the historical books. The two final genres of Old Testament literature, wisdom literature and prophets, fall within the historical timeline contained within our historical books. In essence, the five books that make up wisdom literature as well as the fifteen Old Testament prophets were

---

[28] Bill T. Arnold, "1 & 2 Samuel" in *NIV Application Commentary*, ed. Terry C. Muck (Grand Rapids, MI: Zondervan, 2003), 21.

historically sprinkled throughout the historical books. Fundamentally, without the historical books we would not have a *biblical record* of the historical setting of the wisdom literature or the prophets. And, quite frankly, since we *must* be able to place all scripture within a historical context to properly understand and apply it—the historical books are of *critical significance*.

2. to teach theological principles and lessons

The second purpose we're looking at is just as important or *even more important* than the first purpose: the historical books are *not just a mere historical record*. In addition to providing historical context, the historical books are *chocked full of theological principles and lessons that shape our lives today just as much as any other book of the Bible*. "Although these books are called 'historical,' they are very different from history books of today. The descriptions of events in these books are more often concerned with an important religious teaching about God and God's relationship with Israel than they are about the historical facts of the events themselves."[29] In other words, even though the historical books do provide some *historical facts*, the real purpose was to teach ancient Israel *truth* about God. "The Bible in its entirety—including its historical narratives—is not something that is morally neutral ... It demands a response ... a spiritual response."[30]

This concept is especially important to grasp when considering the reality that some believe the historical books, including the New Testament book of Acts, are not intended to teach theology like other biblical books. Under this false understanding, some folks teach that we should not go to these books for theological truth about God as much as we de other parts of scripture—they exist to provide historical context *only*. Thankfully, recent scholarship has addressed this false belief more so than in the past.

Each book of the Bible is intended to teach us about God; therefore, we must engage the historical books as such. Different genres of literature found within the Bible teach us about God *in different ways*. The historical books do so by telling stories, usually in the form of prose.

---

[29] American Bible Society, https://bibleresources.americanbible.org/resource/historical-books, 2023, Philadelphia. Accessed May 4, 2023.
[30] David M. Howard Jr. *An Introduction to the Old Testament Historical Books*. (Chicago: Moody Press, 1993), 48.

In conclusion, the historical books are not the official historical record of God's people during that period. Rather, these books record the *relevant* history needed for a proper theological understanding of what God was doing in the hearts of His ancient people from the death of Moses to the end of the Old Testament. These books contain some of the most beautiful as well as brutally honest stories depicting God's intervention among His people.

Good news: God is still intervening with us contemporaries every day.

Please enjoy as you now begin to look at each of these twelve historical books in more detail. As you look at the breakdown of each book, please remember the purpose is to provide a very brief introduction to each book. I encourage you to dig deeper beyond what you find here.

Joshua

Big Idea
The righteous reap a restful reward.

Author
Authorship is debated among some scholars, but for our purposes we'll simply state it was Joshua. See "Author" for "Deuteronomy" above for more detail.

Original Recipients
The book of Joshua was written to the Israelite descendants of those who conquered the Promised Land.

Date of Writing
Due to so many eyewitness statements in Joshua, it was probably written during the time of the actual events from about 1405 to 1385 BCE but possibly compiled in its current form sometime shortly thereafter.

Historical Setting/Timeline of Events
The book of Joshua picks up where Deuteronomy leaves off and spans about twenty to twenty-five years. Assuming an early date of 1446 BCE for the Exodus, coupled with the forty years of wandering in the desert, the book of Joshua started about 1405 BCE.

Main Characters
Joshua and the people/tribes of Israel as they conquered and settled the Promised Land.

Purpose
The Torah lays the foundation upon which all events in Joshua are built. Therefore, to best understand the purpose of Joshua we must first understand its relationship to the Torah. Without understanding the promises made to Abraham back in Genesis, we cannot have a true understanding of the purpose of Joshua.

After the fall in Genesis 3 and the perpetuating downward spiral of rebellion following it, God steps in at Genesis 12 to provide a solution with

Abraham's lineage. Fundamentally, Abraham was the beginning of God's official response to our sin problem. Through Abraham, God began to grow a family lineage through whom the Messiah would eventually come. As part of the preparation for this Messiah, God promised to give them a land of their own. God's faithfulness in giving them that land is the primary focus of Joshua.

To be clear, we cannot simply assume the main thrust of Joshua is to provide a historical record of Israel conquering the Promised Land. This book, as with every book in the Bible, celebrates God and teaches of His goodness in two main ways.

1. One of God's main characteristics highlighted here is His faithfulness. Generations ago He had made a promise to give His people a homeland—and it is in Joshua that He follows through with His word. The Israelites grasped a very clear image of God's faithfulness as they conquered the land (chapters 1–12) and divided it among the tribes (chapters 13–24).

2. The second purpose was to reiterate to this new generation of Israelites that God is righteous. He was to be followed wholeheartedly if blessings were to be granted. Without going into significant explanation, our Jewish brothers and sisters can help us better understand this point as we consider how they categorized this book in their Jewish canon. "The inclusion of Joshua with the Former Prophets in the Jewish canon shows keen insight into the true function of the book. The author's intention was not to preserve history for its own sake … He wanted to proclaim that Israel was blessed at the time of the Conquest because she was faithful to her God and to His law and that this would be the secret of Israel's success and blessing in every generation."[31] In other words, His people were enjoying success because they were following Him. Unfortunately, this was short-lived, which resulted in the complications found in the next book of the Bible, Judges.

---

[31] Donald H. Madvig, "Joshua," In *The Expositor's Bible Commentary*, vol. 3, ed. Frank E. Gaebelein (Grand Rapids, MI: Zondervan, 1992), 244.

Key Scripture(s) and Theme(s)

"Not one of the good promises which the Lord had made to the House of Israel failed; all came to pass" (Joshua 21:45).

Contemporary Application

1. God is holy and therefore will never tolerate rebellion in our hearts. When Israel took the Promised Land, the folks living there were driven out specifically because of *their* sin and rebellion. However, God plays no favorites and treated the Israelites the same way. When sin was found in the camp, the Conquest was halted until it was remedied (chapter 7). In our lives we must understand that God is to be respected and followed according to His terms. Either we follow Him according to His terms, or we simply don't follow Him at all. There is no middle ground from God's perspective. This has direct application to the twenty-first century today in that so many people want to have it their own way but still believe they are "OK" in God's sight. Sorry, this is not the case, and we'll see that shortly in the book of Judges.

2. God is full of mercy. Despite His "no tolerance" policy regarding rebellion, He is unbelievably merciful to a repentant heart. We see God have mercy even to foreign pagans in the book of Joshua as He spares Rahab and the Gibeonites. So, to those in this generation that choose to follow Him, He extends such a compassionate hand of mercy every time we fail. I am very thankful for this as it seems that my life is a classic example of falling, getting up, falling, getting up, falling, getting up …

When we turn to Him, even in our sin, He is full of grace and mercy. Toward a repentant heart God is sure to stick to His word that "not one of the good promises which the Lord had made to the House of Israel failed; all came to pass" (Joshua 21:45).

And this is exactly why we say *the righteous reap a restful reward.*

Judges

Big Idea

God's discipline is designed for deliverance.[32]

Author

No one knows for sure, but there are two likely options. The Talmud, which is the basis for Jewish law, claims Samuel wrote it, and for our purposes we will stick with tradition and go with this answer. However, while this view is widely accepted by Jewish and Christian leaders, many modern biblical scholars reject this and claim it was written by a Babylonian exile shortly after 586 BCE along with Deuteronomy, Joshua, Samuel, and Kings—all known as Deuteronomic History. See "Author" under "Deuteronomy" for more detail.

Original Recipients

The original recipient is ancient Israel during the time of the Kings. See "Date of Writing" for more information.

Date of Writing

"Several factors show that the author lived and wrote during the early monarchy."[33] We know this because of the very last verse of the book, which states: "In those days Israel had no king ..." So, we can legitimately assume it was written after their first king began reigning, otherwise why would a king be mentioned? Saul became king around 1046 BCE, so Judges would have been written sometime shortly thereafter but likely before King Solomon's death in 931 BCE.

Historical Setting/Timeline of Events

The events found in the book of Judges take place immediately following the twenty- to twenty-five-year period described in the preceding book, Joshua. It "embraces the period of 350 years, from the death of

---

[32] Paul R. House, *Old Testament Theology* (Downers Grove, IL: Intervarsity Press, 1998), 214.

[33] Herbert Wolf, "Judges," in *The Expositor's Bible Commentary*, vol. 3, ed. Frank E. Gaebelein (Grand Rapids, MI: Zondervan, 1992), 378.

Joshua to the rise of Samuel as a prophet of the Lord."[34] So when one does the math, Judges began approximately 1385–1380 BCE and concluded roughly three and a half centuries later.

A specific timeline showing dates served for each judge is very difficult. In the words of John H. Walton: "The chronology of the judges is very uncertain because we are not told where overlapping occurs."[35]

The children of Israel had settled the land in Joshua but now in Judges they had ignored God's call to remain faithful. They had become stagnant in their faith, adopting a *relaxed version* of the commitment required by God. This resulted in three and a half centuries of turmoil, disgrace, and instability.

Main Characters

The twelve judges as well as the Israelites to whom they were providing rescue serve as the main characters. The twelve judges were:

1. Othniel from the tribe of Judah (3:7–11)
2. Ehud from the tribe of Benjamin (3:12–30)
3. Shamgar, tribe uncertain (3:31)
4. Deborah from the tribe of Ephraim (4:1–5:31)
5. Gideon from the tribe of Manasseh (6:1–8:35)
6. Tola from the tribe of Issachar (10:1–2)
7. Jair from the tribe of Gilead (10:3–5)
8. Jephthah from the tribe of Gilead (10:6–12:7)
9. Ibzan from the tribe of Judah (12:8–10)
10. Elon from the tribe of Zebulun (12:11–12)
11. Abdon from the tribe of Ephraim (12:13–15)
12. Sampson from the tribe of Dan (13:1–16:31)

Purpose

The children of Israel had conquered the Promised Land. Upon doing so, God instructed them not to intermingle or intermarry with the foreign

---

[34] C. F. Keil and F. Delitzsch, *Biblical Commentary on the Old Testament*—vol. 2: Joshua, Judges, Ruth, 1 and 2 Samuel. (Edinburgh: T. & T. Clark, 1857), 1.

[35] John H. Walton, *Chronological and Background Charts of the Old Testament* (Grand Rapids, MI: Zondervan, 1994), 26.

nations surrounding them. They were also instructed not to worship their gods. However, after the death of their leader Joshua, they did exactly what they were told not to do. This led to severe spiritual and moral decay.

To restore His people, God turned them over to foreign invaders, using these nations as the rod of discipline to bring His people back into relationship. Under foreign rule the Israelites would cry out to God in repentance. In response, God would raise an individual to lead them out of bondage. Once out of bondage, the people would again turn their back on God causing the cycle to repeat. Repentance would come and so another leader would be raised to lead the rebellion causing peace again in the land. This cycle occurred twelve times in the book of Judges. Each of the twelve leaders God raised to bring His people out of foreign rule were called judges.

Key Scripture(s) and Theme(s)

Two recurring phrases appear throughout this book as each new judge is introduced. The first phrase highlights the apostasy or falling away from God as it states: "The people of Israel did what was evil in the sight of the Lord ... and He sold them into the hands of ..."

The second phrase highlights their repentance as it states: "But when the people of Israel cried to the Lord, the Lord raised up a deliverer for the people ..." Upon their repentance God would raise a judge to lead them out of foreign domination from their surrounding enemies.

Judges 2:10–23 provides a great summary of this cycle and the recurring phrases.

Contemporary Application

Modern culture and its moral relativism have truly waged war on God and His followers. We have been called to follow God, according to what He decides is best for us. Our opinion is not a consideration to God. However, today's culture has crept in and taught that *we* decide our own morality. This is poison! Lucky for us, our modern moral decay isn't new. We can look at the book of Judges and see the same false perspective pervading in their day over three thousand years ago. This gives us a prescription to follow, a solid path back to God.

The final verse in the book of Judges not only provides us with a clear picture of their mentality but also demonstrates with precise accuracy the society within which we now live: "In those days Israel had no king; everyone did as they saw fit" (Judges 21:25). In essence, Judges teaches us that our modern moral relativism, or "behavior based on human opinions"[36] is to be discarded and disregarded as anti-truth. We do not and cannot define our own standards for living; rather we seek God's guidance through His Word to find the external truth and apply it internally.

The Bible teaches that morality is something external to the human and therefore we are tasked with searching for it, finding it, and then choosing whether we are going to allow this external morality to bring about internal change. However, moral relativism teaches exactly the opposite. Modern society is teaching us that *we* find our *own* individualistic morality by looking inward at ourselves and then applying it outward into the world. This is incredibly dangerous and results in so many sincere but misguided people and societies.

Let's look briefly at one hot topic in our morally relativistic culture today.

Abortion. It's almost incomprehensible that this is debated within the church. In essence, some of us have allowed the world to influence us into believing that murder is acceptable given certain circumstances. How far we have fallen! Suffice it to say that God loves all people, born and unborn, and even gives us a clear scriptural depiction of what He's doing inside a mother before her child is born. Psalm 139:13–14 states: "For you created my inmost being; you knit me together in my mother's womb. I praise you because I am fearfully and wonderfully made; your works are wonderful ..." In contrast to God's Word, our secular culture has attempted to pull truth from within themselves, and it has led to them pulling out the stitching that God had previously knitted together.

So how do we treat this issue? First and foremost, we must accept and embrace those that have committed this act but have fallen at the feet of Christ seeking mercy. We are to fully embrace them, love them, nurture them, and teach them what it means to be forgiven. We cannot have an us/them mentality when thinking of those that have had an abortion

---

[36] Bill T. Arnold and Bryan E. Beyer, *Encountering Biblical Studies, Encountering the Old Testament*, ed. Eugene H. Merrill (Grand Rapids, MI: Baker Book House, 1999), 185.

but are repentant. We are all on even ground—guilty and punishable by death if we are not bathed in God's undeserved mercy. Second, men must be addressed. If we men would step up and fulfill our God-given purpose as fathers, so many issues including abortion would be squelched in magnificent ways. So many times a future mother undergoes abortion because the "dad" left upon finding out the news. What an atrocity! Man up, men! Finally, we must do all we can to stop abortion, most of which must take place on a political level.

May we all look not within ourselves for morality and truth but, instead, look outwardly toward God as we bow a knee in submission. Otherwise, we may have to learn the hard way that *God's discipline is designed for deliverance.*

Ruth

Big Idea

God is working out His great cosmic plan through the everyday normal lives of you and I.

Author

Jewish tradition claims the author was Samuel, but many modern scholars disagree. If the author was not Samuel, we are unsure of authorship.

Original Recipients

The original recipient was the nation of Israel sometime shortly after they received their first king, Saul.

Date of Writing

If Samuel was the author, it was written sometime in his lifetime, 1080–1004 BCE, after the monarch was established with either Saul or David as king.

Historical Setting/Timeline of Events

The book of Ruth opens with the statement "In the days when the judges ruled …" therefore we know it fits chronologically somewhere in the book of Judges. (Judges began approximately 1385–1380 BCE and concluded roughly three and a half centuries later. See "Judges" for more information on the date).

The four chapters of the book of Ruth represent four clear and different scenes, almost set up like a play. Chapter 1 opens with a very big problem. Due to a famine in Bethlehem, a man named Elimelek, his wife, Naomi, and their two sons went to live in Moab. While there, the husband and both sons died, leaving Naomi alone with her two daughters-in-law. Naomi was in dire straits as women could find security only through their husband in that culture. She heard that God had provided relief back in Bethlehem, so she and her two daughters-in-law returned. Naomi attempted to send both of her deceased sons' wives back to Moab so they would have a chance at a new start, but Ruth refused to return. The scene ends with the words: "So Naomi returned from Moab accompanied by Ruth the Moabite, her daughter-in-law, arriving in Bethlehem as the barley harvest was beginning" (Ruth 1:22).

Chapter 2 introduces Boaz, a wealthy relative of Naomi's. A conversation between Ruth and Naomi leads Ruth to go to the fields and "pick up the leftover grain behind anyone in whose eyes I find favor" (Ruth 2:2). She does this and unknowingly goes to a field belonging to Ruth's rich relative, Boaz. He notices Ruth and over the course of several verses asks her not to go to anyone else's field. He then instructs his workers to leave extra grain for her (it was the law in those days for harvesters to leave behind portions of the crop for the poor). At the end of the day Ruth tells Naomi of her adventures, and at this point we are introduced to the concept of "kinsman-redeemer." Boaz was a kinsman-redeemer in the family line of Naomi. This position had several responsibilities, one of which was to reclaim the family's land if it was sold (land in that day could not be permanently sold, only leased for a time. It was the kinsman-redeemer's responsibility to ensure it was returned to the family). However, along with this responsibility came the duty of marrying any widows to bear children to take the name of the deceased husband and thus continue the family name and inheritance rights.

Chapter 3 opens with Naomi and Ruth discussing the need for Ruth to have a home where she would be well provided for—basically she needed a husband. Naomi had obviously put significant thought into the next few actions taken by Ruth. Through a series of strange cultural maneuvers Ruth makes it very clear to Boaz that she is available for marriage. He is overjoyed but told her that another relative had first right, but if this man chose not to redeem, Boaz would be glad to.

Chapter 4 tells of Boaz at the city gate where he confirmed the other relative did not want to redeem. Therefore, Boaz quickly redeemed Naomi's land and married Ruth who then bore a child. These events concluding with a son were so significant in the life of Naomi and Ruth—they had been redeemed from their hopeless state.

Main Characters

God is certainly the main character in this book. Additionally, there are three human main characters around which the story centers: Naomi, Ruth, and Boaz.

Purpose

Though the storyline outlined above is very interesting, we must wait until the conclusion to find its purpose. Here we find a brief but unbelievably important genealogy that gives the entire narrative its purpose in the overarching plan of God. The lineage recorded here tells us very pointedly that Boaz is the great-grandfather of the future King David. This is central as Jesus Christ would be born roughly a thousand years after David's reign as king, arising as the true King from the lineage of David. So in the book of Ruth we are shown a small snippet of God's great plan to save humanity as it was fleshed out in real time and in ordinary real lives.

Key Scripture(s) and Theme(s)

The overarching theme of Ruth isn't found until the very end, and it can be very fleeting to the uninformed reader. The last five verses define the main theme that *God is working out His great cosmic plan through the everyday normal lives of His people.* But this theme is somewhat concealed within the short and simple genealogy that traces these individuals' family line all the way to King David. Though genealogies aren't in and of themselves inspiring, this lineage grants amazing purpose to the short story of Ruth as it dictates that their heritage, bloodline, and struggles would bring about King David and ultimately Jesus Christ.

Contemporary Application

Though we often feel as if our lives are in utter disorganization and chaos, the book of Ruth teaches us that "God is totally and continuously in control of all human events, though in an unperceived way …"[37] You can rest assured that when you feel like there is no meaning to your life, two things are certain.

---

[37] F. B. Huey Jr., "Ruth," in *The Expositor's Bible Commentary,* vol. 3, ed. Frank E. Gaebelein (Grand Rapids, MI: Zondervan, 1992), 512.

1. You are not alone in your feelings when situations in life point toward hopelessness or lack of purpose. Everyone feels this way— much of their life. The struggle to claw at progress in your life is shared by *all*, no matter how "together" others may appear. Do you think Naomi and Ruth were overjoyed with glee as they were losing their husbands and children to death? Do you think their hearts were full of purpose as they trekked back to Bethlehem to make a grim attempt at carving out a hopeless existence? Do you think they were feeling honored to survive and persist in what appeared to be an exercise in futility? You are not alone, my friend. The old REM song wraps it up quite nicely with the lyrics "everybody hurts."

2. The second application from this is that even though life seemed hopeless to Naomi and Ruth, all throughout their scraping by, God had a plan. Though their situation seemed grim, bland, unimportant and uninteresting to them, God was very concerned and involved. He was taking their impossible situation and using it to bring about the most important human being to walk the Earth, Jesus Christ. So when you feel as if your situation is full of gloom, please hold on to the fact that God certainly has a plan, and it *is* being fleshed out in your life even in the hardest of times. God's ways are strange to us because we do not see the future result. But God is certainly parading at the end of time cheering for you. Until we see Him, we are to hold on tight and keep pushing. We don't know what He knows. But we can rest assured He is turning us into a beautiful piece of His intricate plan!

Ultimately, we can rest easy knowing that regardless of the roller coaster of life, we are *all* a part of God's great plan. So many questions in life leave us feeling like we just don't know what to do. God allows us to experience these questions and for good reasons. First, these questions keep us on the path searching for God. Second, and much more importantly, God often leaves the questions unanswered because He knows that while we *can* handle the questions, we can't handle the answers.

Back then God used the normal, mundane, sweaty, arduous lives of Naomi, Ruth, and Boaz to bring about Christ. Now, God is using our normal, mundane, sweaty, arduous lives to broadcast that same Christ into the lives of those we encounter. It's all part of His great plan. So, for all the single mothers or stay-at-home moms out there that struggle just to see purpose, your purpose is very real! You never know who you're raising! For the father that works so hard to bring home a measly paycheck that is taxed to no end, please know your work is not in vain! For the businessman or businesswoman that finds the cutthroat world of business unappealing and often sickening, just know that you are there for a purpose.

Each of us have said to ourselves, "I sure didn't think life would turn out this way." Aren't you glad it's turning out how God planned instead of how you planned? Aren't you glad that *God is working out His great cosmic plan through the everyday normal lives of you and I*?

1 and 2 Samuel

Big Idea

Obedience is better than sacrifice.

Author

Samuel wrote the first twenty-four chapters of 1 Samuel while Nathan and Gad wrote its remainder as well as the entirety of 2 Samuel. Also, see "Author" under "Deuteronomy" for a different perspective.

Original Recipients

The ancient Israelites during the time of the kings serve as the original recipients of this writing.

Date of Writing

Samuel, the author of the first twenty-four chapters of I Samuel, was born approximately 1080 BCE and died around 1004 BCE. His contribution was written probably in the latter years of his life. Nathan and Gad, who wrote the last seven chapters of I Samuel and the entirety of II Samuel, lived and served around the time of David's reign (1010 to 970 BCE).

Historical Setting/Timeline of Events

First and Second Samuel were originally one work that was later separated. So in the modern Christian Bible, Samuel is represented by two books, but we must treat them as one work if we are to best grasp the purpose and application.

That being said, 1 Samuel covers about seventy years of Israel's history from the birth of Samuel (approximately 1080 BCE) to King Saul's death in battle against the Philistines (approximately 1010 BCE). Second Samuel picks up the chronology with Israel being left without a king and provides a record of how David assumed the throne. It then covers many of the events during his forty-year reign from 1010–970 BCE. (David died in 970 BCE thus ending his reign, but this event is not covered in 2 Samuel).

Main Characters

The main characters are Samuel, King Saul, King David.

Purpose

The Samuels usher in the great institution of the monarchy in Israel. However, to best understand them we must also grasp the premonarch history contained in Joshua and Judges. Throughout Joshua the children of Israel are reminded to obey "the book of the law" (Joshua 1:8, 23:6). For it is only through following God that they were to find success. In the Judges, the Israelites were oppressed by the surrounding nations because they did not follow the orders of Joshua. But God provided rescue when they repented (Judges 2:16, 5:19, 5:31). Thus, the combined theology of Joshua and Judges teaches that *obedience precludes success.* The Samuels continue this message that God's provision is gained through obedience— even with a human king it is still God that brings about victory, success, and prosperity in the Promised Land.[38] Now that the nation was in a new phase (i.e., the monarchy), it was still God that would be their fearless leader and victor. They needed to keep this in mind if they were to find and keep the favor of God.

The book opens with Samuel's birth and quickly depicts him as God's prophet, the man of the hour. Therefore, the personhood of Samuel is key to all other events found in both books. Sometime much later, Samuel's two sons prove to be corrupt and ineligible to inherit his position of leadership. Furthermore, threats from other nations began to mount against God's chosen. These two situations resulted in the people crying out for a king to lead them through their tumultuous time.

Demanding a king wasn't wrong of the people—as a matter of fact, God foretold that there would eventually be a monarchy (Genesis 17:6, 35:11, 49:10).[39] Deuteronomy 17:14–20 provides guidelines for when this monarchy would be established:

> When you enter the land the Lord your God is giving
> you and have taken possession of it and settled in it, and

---

[38] Ibid, 555.
[39] Eugene H. Merrill, *Kingdom of Priests* (Grand Rapids, MI: Baker Books, 1996), 189–90.

you say, "Let us set a king over us like all the nations around us," be sure to appoint over you a king the Lord your God chooses. He must be from among your fellow Israelites. Do not place a foreigner over you, one who is not an Israelite. The king, moreover, must not acquire vast numbers of horses for himself or make the people return to Egypt to get more of them, for the Lord as told you, "You are not to go back that way again." He must not take many wives, or his heart will be led astray. He must not accumulate large amounts of silver and gold. When he takes the throne of his kingdom, he is to write for himself on a scroll a copy of this law, taken from that of the Levitical priests. It is to be with him, and he is to read it all the days of his life so that he may learn to revere the Lord his God and follow carefully all the words of this law and these decrees and not consider himself better than his fellow Israelites and turn from the law to the right or to the left. Then he and his descendants will reign a long time over his kingdom of Israel.

And this is exactly where the people went wrong. They were wrong in choosing a king because *it wasn't God's timing or God's choice in leadership*. The people of Israel asked for a king, not because they felt it was God's time, but because *they had lost faith in the One True King* to bring them through their problematic future. They desired to seek security and rescue in a man versus the God that secured their rescue from Egypt.

Despite their wrong motives, Saul is made king. He miserably fails by breaking several of the commands in the reference to Deuteronomy above. His kingship ended in catastrophic fashion as he committed suicide while in battle against the Philistines (1 Samuel 31:1–4).

Welcome to the stage God's original choice for King—the young David. Though David was God's choice, he still had many failures—specifically highlighted in his affair with Bathsheba and the murder of her husband (2 Samuel 11:1–27). Despite his imperfections, his heart was still bent toward God in a way that led God to bring the new kingdom to success—a world power, affluent and bright.

As one sifts through the history found in 1 and 2 Samuel, it can be clearly determined that those who abandon God's directives will find failure lurking in the shadows. In contrast, those who navigate through their imperfections with true and real repentance, regardless of the depth of their failure, will find the blessing of God.

Key Scripture(s) and Theme(s)

First Samuel 15:22 confirms and wraps up the Big Idea of the Samuels in a neat and nice single verse. Leading up to this verse Saul had destroyed the Amalekites as God instructed, but he didn't fully carry out the mission. He was told to kill everything including the animals, but he took them for himself instead. Samuel called him out, causing Saul to backpedal by saying he was going to sacrifice them to God. Samuel responded by saying in 15:22: "Does the Lord delight in burnt offerings and sacrifices as much as in obeying the Lord? To obey is better than sacrifice, and to heed is better than the fat of rams."

Just as in most of the previous books, it's very clear that at this point in Israel's history He was still teaching them obedience. These books follow along the continuous Old Testament theme that obedience to God leads to His blessings, but disobedience leads to a dreaded future.

Contemporary Application

Two main applications stem from 1 and 2 Samuel. The first comes from analyzing the nation of Israel, and the second from a compare/contrast of kings Saul and David. Please note how both applications tie back into and affirm the Big Idea.

1. Analyzing the nation of Israel.

The children of Israel had chosen to step out of God's will by demanding a king. The demand in and of itself wasn't wrong—they were wrong because of their motive and timing. They decided to put their trust in an earthly king to guide them through their questionable future instead of continuing to trust the One True King.

So this begs the question: What or who are you trusting in when hard times are on the horizon? Is God enough from your perspective? If

He's not, then a proper view of God is seriously lacking. He created the entire cosmos by simply speaking it into existence. He led the Israelites from Egyptian slavery. He brought about His Son to make a way for you to experience eternal peace. And, not least of all, He consistently provides for His people of contemporary times in the same manner He provided for His people of ancient times.

We humans can be entirely fickle. We have a proclivity to follow God in the good times but trying to take control in the bad times. This is natural to us, but it is *completely* illogical! May you be encouraged to become more self-aware of your own inconsistencies in your trust and obedience toward God. For blessings follow those who trust and obey Him, but curses befall the degenerates that take serious difficulties into their own hands. May God always find you trusting Him and Him alone through questionable and difficult times.

2. Comparing/contrasting King Saul and King David.

Though asking for a king wasn't necessarily the wrong thing to do, the Israelites chose the wrong king for the wrong reason at the wrong time. At the end of the day, the heart of King Saul was not bent toward God. Though he had moments of positive expression toward God, I personally see those moments as a farce of some sort—almost like that's just what he was supposed to do as dictated by his culture. How sad it is that many of us, me included, do our "church" thing half-heartedly simply because that's just part of what we think we're supposed to do. I am certainly guilty from time to time, and that is a shame. God has saved me from an immensely horrible destiny far beyond my imagination, and I sometimes return the immeasurable grace with nonchalant disgrace.

David, in contrast to Saul, is referred to in scripture as a man after God's own heart. Because of this, David was so much more successful than Saul, but he also had failures equal to or greater than that of Saul. So why is Saul condemned while David is praised and allowed to carry the lineage of Christ? I think the answer can be found by comparing Saul's response versus David's response when called out for their sins. First Samuel 15 records the story of Saul being told to completely kill the enemy. Everything was to die including the animals. However, Saul took the animals for himself. When Samuel addressed him by asking: "Why did you not obey the Lord?" he replied with "But I did obey the Lord ... I completely destroyed the Amalekites ... *the soldiers* took the sheep and cattle ... *to sacrifice them* to the Lord *your* God. Saul completely lied. He said: "But I did obey the Lord ..." However, his response also reveals a heart that was indifferent toward God in three ways:

1. He didn't take the blame for his actions but blamed the soldiers instead.
2. He claimed to have allowed the soldiers to do it to sacrifice them to God. This was, in my estimation, a deceptive attempt to cover his sin.
3. In speaking to Samuel, he stated he wanted to sacrifice them to "your" God. This is indicative of his mentality to simply appease the God of Samuel instead of serving Him directly.

David also committed great sin. Second Samuel 11 records his affair with Bathsheba followed by the murder of her husband. We know now that David was certainly a godly man. But think of his life in contemporary terms: today we would put him in prison for life! However, his response to the prophet Nathan was completely opposite to that of Saul's. David's response was simply: "I have sinned against the Lord." Furthermore, part of his punishment was that the son born from the affair would die. So David began mourning his son's death prior to his birth. Yet the instant his son died, he did something so antithetical to the normal response: "he went into the house of the Lord and worshipped" (2 Samuel 12:20). What a heart toward God!

From the response to our sin emerges the truest proclamation of our heart.

Does your heart lean on God through your struggle, or do you distance yourself from Him with lies, coverups, and deception? As we live and lead throughout life, we will either follow in the way of Saul or in the way of David. The choice is completely ours. May you and I truly understand that *obedience is better than sacrifice.*

1 and 2 Kings

Big Idea

Pass or fail. Obedience or disobedience. Faithfulness or unfaithfulness.

Author

Authorship is not known with certainty, but it was probably written or at least compiled by a single individual. Some have suggested that Ezra or Ezekiel wrote it while the Talmud (Jewish tradition) claims "Jeremiah wrote his own book, and the book of Kings, and Lamentations."[40] In the end we are uncertain, but for our purposes we'll stick with tradition and grant Jeremiah authorship.

Original Recipients

The original recipient was the southern kingdom of Judah while they were in or had just come out of Babylonian captivity.

Date of Writing

According to 2 Kings, the Kings were written during the period of the Babylonian exile that took place from 586 BCE to 535 BCE. However, it wasn't finished or distributed until later toward the end or even shortly after the Babylonians allowed King Jehoiachin out of prison in 560 BCE.[41]

Historical Setting/Timeline of Events

First and Second Kings combine to cover over four hundred years of Israel's history from Solomon's reign (970–931 BC) to the end of the monarchy. First Kings opens with the death of King David (970 BC) and continues through Israel's history, recording the reign of Solomon, the death of Solomon and the division of the kingdom after Solomon's death. Second Kings records the events of the captives of the northern kingdom of Israel and the southern kingdom of Judah.

---

[40] Tzvi Hersh Weinreb and Joshua Schreier, eds., *Koren Talmud Bavli, The Noe Edition. Vol. 27: Tractate Bava Batra, Part One. Perek I Daf 15 Amud a* (Jerusalem: Koren Publishers, 2016), 81.

[41] Thomas L. Constable, "1 Kings," in *The Bible Knowledge Commentary: Old Testament*, ed. John F Walvoord and Roy B. Zuck (Wheaton, IL: Victor Books, 1985), 483.

Main Characters

King Solomon, the prophets and the kings of Judah and Israel are the main characters.

Purpose

Much like every Old Testament book, 1 and 2 Kings is all about obedience, faithfulness, and trust in God. Very systematically and with premeditated precision, the author critiques and rates each king on a pass/fail basis from Solomon to the end. These pass/fail grades can be tracked very clearly in scripture as it is said of every king that either "they did evil in the eyes of the Lord" or they "did what was right in the eyes of the Lord."

While the successes and failures of the monarchy period are charted, the *real* purpose of the Kings is to explain *why* each king failed or succeeded. Ultimately, faithfulness to God meant success while unfaithfulness was automatic failure. To state it another way, 1 and 2 Kings *provides a spiritual and religious explanation* for the successes and failures of each king and the nation under their rule. Unfortunately, more kings were disobedient than obedient. Thus we see an undertone focusing on this aspect providing an explanation of the downfall of both nations. Israel fell into Assyrian captivity while Judah fell to the Babylonians.

The sorrow brought on by sin is a serious focus of the Kings.

Key Scripture(s) and Theme(s)

First and Second Kings uses the phrases "He did evil in the eyes of the Lord" and "He did what was right in the eyes of the Lord" to encapsulate the success or failure of each king of Israel and Judah. This clearly drew a line in the sand regarding the themes of obedience, faithfulness, and trust in God.

Contemporary Application

While 1 and 2 Kings originally provided the Old Testament people *the spiritual reason* for the success and failure of each king, we contemporaries now have an even broader perspective contained in the *completed* Word of God. We now place the Kings into a larger context of scripture that the original recipients simply did not have. This gives us a more expounded upon perspective of what God was doing throughout the Kings and the whole of the Old Testament because we now look through the lens of the New Testament.

Why do we see the common theme of obedience and faithfulness toward God throughout every Old Testament book? The answer is something of legends: obedience and faithfulness had to be taught to Old Testament Israel because God was bringing about the ultimate plan of salvation in Jesus Christ through them!

Some may ask why their obedience and faithfulness was so vital to the success of God's plan. There are theological responses to this question, but let's just look at the very practical illustration of high school football. The players on the field are responsible for executing the play, but the coach makes the call. If the players ignore the coach, they guarantee their own loss—and so it was with Israel. Somehow, in God's great wisdom, He knew the people had to follow His call for the win to take place—for His game plan to succeed. And so it is with us. We must follow the play called by our Creator.

So where is your obedience? Where is your faithfulness. Where is your trust in Him? If you were given a pass/fail score like the kings, where would you stand? To be clear, we *are* given a pass/fail grade, and it's based upon our obedience, faithfulness and trust in His Son Jesus Christ.

If you're anything like me, you are constantly fighting the flesh to remain obedient, faithful and maintain trust in God. Some days are better than others but regardless, we keep trying. We don't quit. We don't back down. We get back up and keep going, period. No excuses. We push forward with a grit and a mental fortitude that says, "I'm prepared to die before I quit serving Jesus." We strive for the prize – we strive for the passing score by turning over our wins AND our losses to Christ. On our bad days when we fall, we kiss the feet of Christ before rising… for He is certainly standing there with outstretched arms to lift us. On our good days we go ahead and kiss His feet anyway as we bow in reverence thanking Him for victory.

Back in the days of the Kings, God was fleshing out His plan of salvation for the world, and He continues to do the same today. He used the Old Testament people to bring about Christ, and He continues to use you and I to do the same in our own lives and the lives of our contemporaries.

The only difference between us and the Old Testament people is that they were on one side of Christ in history, and we're on the other.

May God's grace be with you as you strive for obedience, faithfulness, and trust in God and our great savior Jesus Christ. Please remember, with God it's *pass or fail. Obedience or disobedience. Faithfulness or unfaithfulness.*

1 and 2 Chronicles

Big Idea
Repentance results in restoration.

Author
Early Jewish tradition considers Ezra as the author of the Chronicles[42] but recent scholarship questions this belief. For our purposes we'll consider Ezra the author of at least part of it. However, if our view is incorrect, we can be certain the author was at least a contemporary of Ezra.

Original Recipients
The Chronicles were written to God's people over a hundred years after the original recipients of the Kings. The post-exilic Jews of the mid to early 400s BCE had returned to Jerusalem when the king of Persia allowed their return under Zerubbabel, Nehemiah, and Ezra.[43] These folks were facing very troubling and discouraging times so the Chronicler writes to these people.

Date of Writing
The Chronicles were written about a century after the Kings were written[44] so that gives us a date somewhere in the mid to early 400s BCE.

Historical Setting/Timeline of Events
As the books of the Kings provide focus on God's judgment toward a rebellious people, the Chronicler provides balance in showing God's salvation extended to the repentant. The people of God to whom the Chronicles were originally written were in absolute and dire straits. The glories of David and Solomon's Israel were long gone (five centuries between David/Solomon and the original audience of Chronicles). Assyria had

---

[42] Tzvi Hersh Weinreb and Joshua Schreier, eds., *Koren Talmud Bavli, The Noe Edition. Vol. 27: Tractate Bava Batra, Part One. Perek I Daf 15 Amud a* (Jerusalem: Koren Publishers, 2016), 81.

[43] Bill T. Arnold and Bryan E. Beyer, *Encountering Biblical Studies, Encountering the Old Testament*, ed. Eugene H. Merrill (Grand Rapids, MI: Baker Book House, 1999), 252.

[44] Ibid.

carried the northern kingdom of Israel into captivity never to return (721 BCE). The Babylonians had carried off the southern kingdom of Judah into captivity of which only a remnant remained (586 BCE). During the time of the Chronicles' original audience, the Babylonian exile had ended just a little more than a century prior due to Persia conquering Judah's captors, the Babylonians. Therefore, by default, Persia assumed command of all of Babylon's captives, including God's people. Fortunately, Persia was much more relaxed in their foreign policies and allowed the Jews to return to their homeland if they continued to submit to Persian authority.

Though they were free from exile, they were a far cry from the nation they had once been. Discouragement permeated the air, and doubt had dug a solid foothold into the hearts of the people. Their expectation that the Messiah would arrive and provide rescue was left unfulfilled. Had God abandoned them? Was the Davidic covenant null and void? The faithful followers of God were in peril … and though the Messiah wouldn't come for over four hundred more years, *the Chronicles were just what they needed.* It taught them that the ultimate plan of God was not in failure mode— they were guaranteed to find God's success in repentance.

Main Characters

The events recorded in the Chronicles were a glance back into the past. King David is the main character of 1 Chronicles while Solomon and all kings that followed him are the main characters of 2 Chronicles.

Purpose

Though the Chronicles cover much of the same history as that of the Samuels and Kings, the Chronicles retell Israel's history with a completely different purpose in mind. The author gently took the hand of the tattered faithful and traced God's covenant from its beginning to their present day. By doing so he showed how God had remained faithful in the past and would continue to do so despite their current fragmented and shattered situation. The Chronicler extended *a soft hand* of hope, optimism, and confidence to a people that had been wrecked from centuries of defeat and disappointment. "Malachi, Ezra and Nehemiah consider it their job to raise the people's enthusiasm for serving the Lord, and the Chronicler also writes with this goal in mind."[45]

The Chronicles were written with a gentle tone and a soft touch.

Key Scripture(s) and Theme(s)

The famous passage of 2 Chronicles 7:14 serves as a great focal point for the entire writing. "If my people, who are called by my name, will humble themselves and pray and seek my face and turn from their wicked ways, then I will hear from heaven, and I will forgive their sin and will heal their land." The people were suffering from their sin. All they had to do was repent.

Contemporary Application

Hard times come to us all ... sometimes not our fault but other times certainly due to our own sin. Our reaction to God in those hard times caused by our sin will determine our outcome. Rebellion leads to defeat, but repentance leads to restoration. This is why we must obey God and His Word. It is impossible to break God's law, but we do break ourselves against it. The Chronicler illustrates this to the broken and defeated people of Israel, and the same applies to us today.

Our earthly fatherhood and motherhood serve as a perfect example. I've seen so many examples in public of horrible, overbearing, domineering, and ill-willed parents that obviously consider their children as nothing more than mere stumbling blocks. Hardly anything is more disgraceful, and those parents *will* be held accountable by God! Though bad parenting is evil in and of itself, it also has another repercussion on the children beyond the initial abuse itself. Our parenting skills directly form our children's view of God. If I'm cruel and callous toward my son, he will begin to believe that God is also cruel and callous toward him. However, if I cherish my son and raise him the way God desires, my son will grow up with a positive view of God. If I bring praise *and* discipline into his life in a biblical manner, he will view God's praise and discipline from that same biblical perspective. God's discipline is always redemptive in nature, and so we should mimic that redemption with our children as we discipline

---

[45] Paul R. House, *Old Testament Theology* (Downers Grove, IL: Intervarsity Press, 1998.), 524.

them. God's nature is not mean-spirited, and neither is His discipline—He is always good to us. So, every time I discipline my son, it always concludes with an embrace. God is the same with us.

So, as the message of the Chronicles is one of encouragement, so you too should be encouraged today! If you find yourself suffering due to sin, the only real option is repentance. Despite your sin, God will redeem you! He is not an abusive father looming overhead just waiting and wanting to beat us when we disappoint Him! Rather, in our sinful moments, He is a weeping Father that simply wants His children to return to Him. For it is only in returning to Him that His best is dispersed into our lives.

Because He is a Good Father, we must be reminded that God cannot and will not negotiate with His creation. If we are to experience His best for us, we must submit. It sounds paradoxical on the surface, but it is the very goodness of God that led Israel into hard times when they sinned. It is also His goodness that leads *us* into hard times when we sin. God's discipline is the best tool to restore our relationship with Him. He knows what's best and will use correction to return us to Him. Unfortunately, brokenness is sometimes the only means that shakes our stubborn nature and pulls from within us a repentant heart.

We should not assume that all hard times come to us because of our sin. We live in a fallen world where bad things happen to good people all the time. Nonetheless, we know when we're in sin. We know what sin looks like, and we know what *we look like in it*. So, if that's where you are today, the best thing to do is repent, return, and enjoy the blessed life God desires. It's that simple. This doesn't mean that all will be easy, but it does mean that we will have God's smile of approval.

And really ... isn't that the point of it all anyway—to have God's smile of approval upon our lives?

Stay strong. Be blessed. Never forget that *repentance results in restoration.*

The Chronicles were written by a saddened heavenly Father with a soft tone and a gentle touch. Will you return?

Ezra-Nehemiah

Big Idea

External transformation must be accompanied by internal transformation.

Author

Although Ezra and Nehemiah are considered two books in most modern Bibles, they were originally a single work. Jewish tradition claims that Ezra wrote Ezra-Nehemiah along with the Chronicles.[46] However, this is almost certainly incorrect. Though Ezra and Nehemiah wrote certain sections (their own recorded memoirs in Ezra 7:27–9:15 and Nehemiah 1:17–5, 12:27–43, 13:4–31), the books as we now have them were compiled, edited, and further expounded upon by another individual later in Jewish history sometime in the mid to late 400s BC.[47]

Original Recipients

Ezra-Nehemiah was originally written to the Jews of the restoration. The events of Ezra-Nehemiah cover over a century as it encouraged its recipients to continue the work after returning from exile to rebuild their homeland.

Date of Writing

See "Author" above.

Historical Setting/Timeline of Events

Though our modern Bibles separate these books into two books, Ezra and Nehemiah were originally one work. This single work was written to "record the last events, chronologically, in the Old Testament period."[48]

---

[46] Tzvi Hersh Weinreb and Joshua Schreier, eds., *Koren Talmud Bavli, The Noe Edition. Vol. 27: Tractate Bava Batra, Part One. Perek I Daf 15 Amud a* (Jerusalem: Koren Publishers, 2016), 81.

[47] Bill T. Arnold and Bryan E. Beyer, *Encountering Biblical Studies, Encountering the Old Testament*, ed. Eugene H. Merrill (Grand Rapids, MI: Baker Book House, 1999), 270–71.

[48] David M. Howard, Jr. *An Introduction to the Old Testament Historical Books* (Chicago: Moody Press, 1993). 273.

This chronology is best understood in the context of the shifting world powers at the time.

Starting in 605 BCE and following through to the destruction of the temple in 586 BCE, Babylon had conquered Judah and scattered most of the people throughout their kingdom. They allowed only the poor and unskilled to remain to work the land. In 539 BCE,[49] Persia conquered Babylon, thus inheriting all their captives including God's people. Ezra-Nehemiah picks up the storyline shortly after Persia conquered Babylon. Under Persia's rule, three waves of Jews were allowed to return to their homeland. The first wave centered on those who arrived under Zerubbabel's leadership. In 458 BCE[50] Ezra brought the second wave followed by Nehemiah shortly after with the final wave.

Each of the three leaders had different goals in mind but, unfortunately, each of the three phases ended in anticlimactic fashion. As a matter of fact, from the perspective of the Jews in that period, the morale was possibly even worse at the end of the return than before. The Jews thought their return was as significant as that of the Exodus—as God fulfilling His prophetic word. Though "the majority of the exilic community may have settled in comfortably in Babylon ... those with an eye to the eternal purposes of God saw ... a sure sign that God was not through with His people; they had a redemptive role yet to play."[51] So with each of the three leaders' goals accomplished, the people became very expectant of the coming Messiah. However, they were only further disappointed as He did not appear. Many external changes were taking place through the triad of exilic returns, but inward change was still lacking—thus we have our "Big Idea" above: external transformation must be accompanied by internal transformation.

Main Characters

The main characters are Zerubbabel, Ezra, Nehemiah and the Jews that returned with them from Babylonian exile after Persia conquered Babylon.

---

[49] John Bright, *Jeremiah*, Anchor Bible (Garden City, NY: Doubleday, 1965), 160–61.
[50] Eugene H. Merrill, *Kingdom of Priests* (Grand Rapids, MI: Baker Books, 1996), 492.
[51] Ibid., 475.

Purpose

Ezra-Nehemiah was written as a form of encouragement to the Jews who had slowly returned to Jerusalem. It pushed them to remain faithful to their continued work. They were, over the course of over a hundred years, supposed to continue the postexilic efforts to rebuild the city of Jerusalem and its temple. Through intense opposition and unfulfilled hopes of the arrival of the Messiah, they needed to be reminded that they were to do their part, regardless of the outcome.

The book is recorded as a triad of events centering on the characters of Zerubbabel, Ezra, and Nehemiah. With each of their efforts succeeding, the anticipation of the arriving Messiah would churn the hearts of the people. However, when the Messiah did not appear, they would fall back into a state of national depression.

The purpose of Ezra-Nehemiah was to remind the people, and us today, that external change must be accompanied by internal change. In other words, the external changes being brought about by rebuilding Jerusalem and the temple were to be reflective of the internal spiritual change of God's people in Ezra and Nehemiah's day. This was not always the case.

Key Scripture(s) and Theme(s)

1. External transformation must accompany internal transformation. We see this throughout both books as the people were hoping for their external work to bring about the Messiah.
2. God works as He sees fit in this world—and uses pagan kings and nations as He sees fit (Ezra 1:1).

Contemporary Application

Just a small handful of years ago, our pastor led our church through a building program. Our needs were exceeding capacity and a much-needed building was erected. In this building we have a giant multipurpose room with an incredible stage and seating area. Here we have services, meals, events, etc. We also have a commercial kitchen in which to prepare very tasty meals. Furthermore, our children's program has been greatly improved with an incredible designation upstairs. And to top it off, we have the most up-to-date electronics that provides a context for us to broadcast the gospel in the most professional of ways. That being said, during the building of the project our pastor reminded us many times that it's only a building. We were told many times that if hearts aren't changed, our work would be in vain. Watching our pastor say that as he sat in sweat from head-to-toe toiling through electrical wiring made a significant impact on me. We can have the greatest buildings, the greatest programs, and the greatest external influence, but if lives aren't changed, we are simply not a part of God's great plan.

The Jews, during the time of Ezra-Nehemiah, expected God's presence to fall on them at the completion of the temple much like He did in the days of old. But it didn't happen. They expected their efforts to usher in the Messiah, but it didn't happen. What were they lacking? Many problems existed in the hearts of the Jews during the reconstruction of their postexilic period. Their city and temple were rebuilt (albeit not to their former glory). They expected God to bring about the Messiah based solely on this external change. However, God's timing didn't call for the Messiah to arrive for another four to five centuries—long after these people would be dead and gone. What were they to do?

What are you to think and how are you to live when God's timing isn't your timing? Ultimately, all we can do in this life is allow Him to continue to transform our inward parts and remain faithful to God regardless of our perspective. Thus, we have our Big Idea above: *external transformation must be accompanied by internal transformation.*

Your heart and my heart must undergo a spiritual surgeon's work if we are to find success as God planned. However, considering our failures, His ultimate plan continued through the days of Ezra-Nehemiah and hasn't stopped progressing through the modern era. Eventually God brought about the Messiah, and He is still broadcasting His message of salvation today.

The people of Ezra-Nehemiah had a part to play in God's redemptive work, though not always fun or easy. Likewise, you and I also have a part to play in the same work. We're fulfilling the same plan roughly twenty-four to twenty-five hundred years after the folks of Ezra-Nehemiah. And just as it was true in their day, it's true in our day—*external transformation must be accompanied by inward transformation.*

God holds all of history in His hands, and we are to remain faithful, allowing Him to bring about internal change as we fulfill our small slice of His history of salvation.

Esther

Big Idea

God has not called us to be bystanders.

Author

The identity of the author is ultimately unknown. However, the great historian Josephus named the author as Mordecai[52] and the Talmud claim the authors are the men of the Great Synagogue.[53]

Original Recipients

The original recipients would have been the members of the Jewish community after the Babylonian captivity and death of King Xerxes (464 BCE).

Date of Writing

"The earliest possible date for the writing of the book would be some time after Xerxes's death (464 BCE), since his death seems to be presumed by the summary of his reign in 10:2."[54]

Historical Setting/Timeline of Events

After the captivity of Judah by the Babylonians in 605 BC, the Persians moved in and conquered the Babylonians. Thus, by default, the Persians inherited all the Babylonian captives including God's people. The story of Esther takes place in Susa, the capital of Persia, and began in 483 BCE between the first return from captivity under Zerubbabel and the second return under Ezra.[55]

---

[52] David M. Howard Jr. *An Introduction to the Historical Books* (Chicago: Moody Press, 1993), 316.

[53] Tzvi Hersh Weinreb and Joshua Schreier, eds., *Koren Talmud Bavli, The Noe Edition.* vol. 27: *Tractate Bava Batra, Part One. Perek I Daf 15 Amud a* (Jerusalem: Koren Publishers, 2016), 81.

[54] David M. Howard Jr. *An Introduction to the Historical Books* (Chicago: Moody Press, 1993), 317.

[55] Bill T. Arnold and Bryan E. Beyer, *Encountering Biblical Studies, Encountering the Old Testament*, ed. Eugene H. Merrill (Grand Rapids, MI: Baker Book House, 1999), 272.

Main Characters

Though God's name is never mentioned, He is clearly the main character of this book. As for human characters, the beautiful story centers around a woman named Esther.

Purpose

God is never mentioned in this book, which has led many folks throughout the centuries to find no place for it in the Bible. However, God clearly revealed Himself in its beautifully and artfully articulated storyline. While God is never mentioned, it is undeniably clear that He was orchestrating the solution to an intense problem long before it even began.

Through a series of many improbable and impossible coincidences, a young Jewish woman named Esther ascends to the throne and becomes queen of Persia, illustrating "how the faithfulness and courage of one Jew made a difference in the world in which she lived."[56] Our storyline involves Esther, who was simply a young Jewish woman living in Babylonian exile. Persia had overtaken Babylon and inherited her captive, the southern kingdom of Judah to which Esther belonged. The events center on Esther as she was living in Persia's capital city of Susa along with her uncle Mordecai.

In contrast to the simple Jewish life of Esther, a lady named Vashti was King Xerxes's wife, the Persian queen. One day she found herself summoned by the king, but she refused to appear. So, King Xerxes banished her and replaced her with Esther.

Shortly thereafter, Esther's uncle Mordecai refused to bow down to a Persian official named Haman. This infuriated Haman, so he plotted not only to kill Mordecai but also to kill all Jews. This was made Persian law, which could not be reversed, leaving the city and people of God in utter shock and terror. However, Mordecai spoke with Esther and told her that she had been placed in her position of influence "for such a time as this." So through a series of celebrations she organized for the king and Haman, she revealed the evil plot and Haman as its leader.

To sum it up, the law could not be reversed, but the king issued another edict allowing the Jews to fight back. And that is exactly what

---

[56] Ibid., 264.

they did. Extreme victory was celebrated by God's people, and that victory is still celebrated to this day as the festival of Purim.

Esther had a choice to make. She could have attempted to save herself and not reveal her identity to the king, or she could chance death and make a stand for her people. Thankfully, she made a stand.

Key Scripture(s) and Theme(s)
1. God's victory calls for celebration! Esther 9:20–32 outlines the festival of Purim that is still celebrated today! This is the celebration of God rescuing His people from anti-Semitic extermination.
2. Even though God may seem absent, He is always working in detailed fashion in and through the lives of His people.
3. When duty calls, we'd better step up. In Esther 4 we see a nervous queen worried about losing her life by approaching the king without being summoned. To approach the king without a summons demanded an automatic death penalty unless the king waived it. Mordecai replied by telling her that she need not feel comfortable in the palace because death would come to her too if her people were exterminated. Then he concluded in 4:14 by saying: "And who knows but that you have come to your royal position for such a time as this?" She stepped up.

Contemporary Application
Esther teaches us that God is always in control (sovereign) even when it seems as if He is silent and distant. His name is never mentioned in the book of Esther, but His presence is clear and active! So, the question poses itself to you and I: Do we trust God to direct the affairs of life even when we cannot sense Him?

We need to understand something very clearly about God as taught in Esther: He is *always* in control. There is never a second that goes by that He hasn't *personally notated*. There isn't a tear that falls to the ground without Him recording it. There isn't a single event that takes place that catches Him off guard! Even when we are distant from Him, lost in the consequences of our sin, we are still at the forefront of God's mind. He always has a redemptive plan that He will carry out in the lives of His people *today*.

Due to what seems like God's absence at times, many good, faithful followers of Jesus have asked, "Why are you so silent?!" or "Where are you, God?!" These questions are certainly OK to ask as they serve as a representation of the legitimate human emotions created by God. As a matter of fact, the Psalms convey great men of God asking these questions repeatedly. Therefore, we should ask our questions reverently, *knowing* that He is always in control even when it *feels* like He isn't.

The very harsh reality is that we live in a world where many times it seems as if He doesn't care. So much violence, sickness, disease, divorce, death, and pain piled on top of pain … Is He really there, and does He really care? If you could ask Esther, she would likely respond by shaking her head in empathy and simply affirming that He is here and in control. She would also likely encourage us to join them in the festival of Purim and celebrate! As noted above, the very events contained within Esther led to the Jewish festival of Purim. Each year the Jewish people set aside two days to celebrate their escape from the national slaughter outlined in Esther—and they hold this rescuing to be just as significant as that of the Exodus!

So as you deal with difficulty in life, remember that God is absolutely and unequivocally in control. He has no rival! Even amid tragedy when God seems silent, we still have reason to celebrate. God's Word teaches us, through Esther, that when our emotions tell us God is absent, those emotions are wrong.

Our celebration is never meant to dismiss the intense gravity of life's most severe tragedies. Yet, our celebration is meant to correct our perception of our earthly issues in light of our heavenly Father and the home He has prepared.

A second application from Esther is the *personal acceptance of individual responsibility upon God's call to duty*. His purposes will prevail whether we heed the call or not. So, it's best if we listen and obey the first time. God is always in control and therefore provides whatever solution He chooses—and sometimes *you* are that solution. Folks, we are followers of Christ, which means we are His representative in this world. We have a commitment to the call of the Creator. Whether the mission He gives us individually is considered great or small in our eyes, it is still the mission He has given us, and we are obligated to step up. Although it's unlikely that God will need us to step up to save the lives of an entire people group, our mission is no less important!

Simply crossing paths with someone in need is enough reason to become involved.

God has not called us to be bystanders.

CHAPTER 8

Wisdom Literature

Added information inevitably leads to new questions.

The more we learn about any given topic in life, the more we realize how little we really know. With anything in life, the mountain of questions we have continually grows in proportion to the expansion of our knowledge—*knowledge gained is questions gained*. We've all been in circumstances when the answer to one question only opened the flood gates to several more.

Before we were given the Bible, we simply didn't have as many questions. However, the explosion of knowledge God gave us about Himself in the Bible led humanity down a path of questions that seem to be universal to humanity. And it is this very set of universal questions that serves as the foundation of Old Testament wisdom literature.

Humanity has gathered up, in the conscience and unconscious mind, a set of universal questions that didn't exist prior to understanding God according to how He has revealed Himself in scripture. For example, prior to knowing that God was all-loving and all-powerful as revealed to us in the Bible, we didn't approach the question "Why does bad stuff happen to good people" with quite the finger-pointing with which it is now typically addressed. Without the concept of a good, loving and all-powerful God, we could only assume that life just simply was what it was and bad stuff happens sometimes. But now that our knowledge about God has grown, and we know He cares deeply for us and *also* has the power to intervene, we are led to question deeply: "Hey, if He cares so much and has the power to stop evil, why am I suffering?"

This universal question of evil is dealt with most directly in the book of Job, but four other books comprise this genre called Wisdom Literature: Psalms, Proverbs, Ecclesiastes, and Song of Songs. Each of these five books ask their own set of questions from differing perspectives. Yet the goal of each book is the same: to convey godly wisdom to humanity. *They teach us how to live good lives as we address the difficult questions common to humankind.*

Whether we're dealing with the beauty (and sometimes terror) of the Psalms, the question of evil in Job, the meaninglessness of life in Ecclesiastes, the candid imageries of wisdom in Proverbs, or the vivid descriptions of human intimacy found in the Song of Songs, *the overall goal of these books is to provide humankind an opportunity to gain wisdom that can be accessed only through God.*

Wisdom as found in the poetical books is taught from a very different perspective than most other biblical writings. Most of the Bible is to be understood as *God addressing humankind.* However, for much of this genre we find it reversed—based on the knowledge God has revealed to us about Himself in Scripture, hu*mankind is addressing God* with a set of specific and potent questions. C. Hassell Bullock states in his book *An Introduction to the Old Testament Poetic Books*:

> In part, the spokesmen in these five books speak for man to God ... in contrast to the Prophets, who normally speak for God to man ... The spokesmen in these books formulate questions that have lain in man's subconscious mind, often without his having had courage to bring them to the surface.[57]

In essence, wisdom literature (poetic books) confirms that we as incredibly flawed people *have been granted the freedom by the Perfect Creator to express our most haunting questions.* But one must be very careful when accepting the challenge to grapple with these books. While all scripture is equally inspired and important, wisdom literature was specifically designed to lay bare the deepest, darkest questions within the human heart. It addresses our human condition with crystal-clear clarity in a way that the

---

[57] C. Hassell Bullock, *An Introduction to the Old Testament Poetic Books* (Chicago: Moody, 1979, 1988), 19.

other Old Testament genres simply are not equipped to do. To continue quoting Bullock, in one of the most profound statements I have personally read while researching for this book, he explores this idea a bit further:

> One might read the Pentateuch and see only a faint shadow of himself reflected there. The historical books may overwhelm him with facts and events. The Prophets, by some mere chance, may pass him by with their deep convictions and concerns about their own societies and world. But the poetic books will find him wherever he is.[58]

The five books comprising this genre of scripture lead, lure, and long for humanity to find the courage to come close to the edge of our comprehension ... to peer off into the vast darkness ... and bellow, without reservation, our deepest questions and concerns about God and His ways. No human on this Earth could handle the full truth of God if He were to bellow back without reservation. However, He has given us exactly what we need to live a life full of godly wisdom. With God's wisdom, victory is won against life's toughest and most beautiful questions.

Let's take moment and flesh out what this looks like from a Jewish perspective of wisdom literature.

Wisdom Literature According to Jewish Tradition

Remember how I spoke earlier about working in tandem with those of the Jewish tradition? A classic example of this is found in how Judaism approaches wisdom literature. First off, in Jewish circles wisdom literature is comprised of only three books: Job, Proverbs and Ecclesiastes.

To best understand the book of Job, we must first step back and take a good long gaze at the broader background within which it is placed. From the Jewish perspective, Job must be understood in correlation with the two other books of Proverbs and Ecclesiastes. Each of these books address basically the same question: "Is God and life fair?" Or to put it another

---

[58] Ibid., 20.

way: "What is God really like … and how does that affect human life?" In essence, "the doctrine of God is a key issue in Wisdom Literature."[59]

Proverbs deals with this question very optimistically by saying that God is fair, so generally, the righteous succeed and the evil perish. However, the writer of Ecclesiastes steps in, gives a snarky grin behind a tipped hat, and offers a slightly more pessimistic view with a different opinion. This leaves only one option: we must turn to Job for the tiebreaker. But in an unexpected and extremely disappointing fashion, God never truly flips the coin in Job revealing the answer. What we *are* left with at Job's conclusion is so much greater than the answer to this plaguing question. When all is said and done in the book of Job, God answers Job's question of evil and suffering. But He answers it in a very different way than expected. Essentially God tells Job that before he can handle the answer to the question, he must first be able to manage the cosmos. "The prerequisite to sitting down with God and truly understanding what's going on behind the curtain is that we must first be able to successfully create and tend to all of creation at the same time." In essence, God is telling us that we're looking for answers to questions that we simply cannot handle.

Some things are just not for us to know.

Final Thoughts

Proverbs 1:2–3 (NIV) provides the most concrete understanding for the reason why God revealed to us the wisdom literature. That reason is "for gaining wisdom and instruction; for understanding words of insight; for receiving instruction in prudent behavior; doing what is right and just and fair."

Whether you're learning about the problem of evil in Job, the beauty of God's law in the Psalms, avoiding the temptations of youth in Proverbs, dealing with the purpose of life in Ecclesiastes, or learning the proper application of true love between a man and woman in the Song of Songs, we find wisdom as the central theme of this stunningly written genre.

May we grow in the wisdom of God.

---

[59] Ibid., 61.

Job

Big Idea

God can be trusted in spite of tragedy.

Author

"We do not know who the writer was, but his work has witnessed to the spirits of the faithful through the ages that he was divinely inspired."[60]

Original Recipients

As the author and date of writing is unknown, the original audience cannot be specifically identified chronologically. However, as a part of the Bible's wisdom literature, we know it was written to God's ancient people sometime within biblical chronology to add to the body of wisdom literature's main purpose of *providing godly wisdom to God's people.*

Date of Writing

Ultimately no one knows for sure, but suggested dates vary from the time of Moses to the 400s BC.[61]

Historical Setting/Timeline of Events

Nothing is known of Job outside the Bible, but we do know that "he was not an Israelite and showed no knowledge of the covenant between Yahweh and His chosen people."[62] However, one thing we do know is that Job takes place very early on somewhere "east of the Jordan at a time before the emergence of the Hebrews as a nation."[63] So in Job, even though it was written sometime after Moses, it tells a story of the man Job wrestling with a horrendous situation that predates Abraham in Genesis 12.

The first two chapters provide a behind-the-scenes look at Job's hardship as they prepare the reader for the real question of the book: Why do we suffer?

---

[60] Elmer B. Smick, "Job," In *The Expositor's Bible Commentary*, vol. 4, ed. Frank E. Gaebelein (Grand Rapids, MI: Zondervan, 1988), 846.

[61] Ibid., 851.

[62] Ibid., 861.

[63] Ibid., 861.

These two chapters describe a meeting between God and all the angelic beings. In this meeting, Satan presented himself and questioned the authenticity of Job's faithfulness to God. What Satan *actually* did was question God's character. His argument was that Job only served God because God blessed him with riches and protection. If God would only remove His favor and protection, Job would deny Him. So, God gave Satan permission to test Job. And test Job he did.

Satan caused all his livestock to be stolen, his servants to be killed, and his children to die tragically. Job lost everything. Even his wife told him to curse God and die, but Job refused. When this didn't work, Satan received additional permission to strike Job's body. Aching boils appeared sending Job into excruciating pain. But Job continued to praise God.

The next section, chapters 3–37, deal with Job's three friends as they sought to make sense of the mess. Through a series of several discourses between Job and his friends, Job cursed the day of his birth while his friends gave orthodox yet illegitimate reasons why so much tragedy had struck.

Job put God on trial.

And he did it respectfully (1:20–22, 2:10, 7:20, 9:3–4, 9:14–15, 9:32–35, 13:20–25, 16:15–17, 19:25–27, 21:16, 21:22, 23:1–7, 27:1–6, 31:5–8, 40:3–5, 42:1–17).

God responded to being put on trial in the third section, chapters 38–42:6. Here, God showed up and answered Job's questions. However, Job was nowhere even close to prepared for the answer. God responded by turning the tables and putting Job on trial!

He basically asked, through a series of several questions, if Job was there to give Him advice when He created everything. In other words, Job was put in his place. In all this Job remained humble and reverent. God essentially explained to Job that there was a prerequisite to being capable of understanding the question of suffering and evil. That prerequisite was that Job first must be able to create and manage the cosmos. In other words, it's easier to manage the planet and all the constellations than it is to grasp what's really going on behind the curtain regarding why we suffer.

Obviously, there's way more going on beyond what we could ever comprehend.

In the fourth and final section, God blessed Job even more than he had been before his test. He elevated him beyond his previous status. Furthermore, God demonstrated to all Job's family, friends, *and* foes that he committed no sin to deserve the harshness dealt to him.

Main Characters

The main characters are God, Job, and Job's friends.

Purpose

When we fail to view the book of Job through the lens of Jewish understanding, we simply fail to understand it as it was intended. The Jewish canon categorizes Job, Ecclesiastes, and Proverbs to be the only books contained within wisdom literature while we add Psalms and Song of Songs. *Please* go reread the subsection "Wisdom Literature According to Jewish Tradition" in the introduction to wisdom literature for a clearer understanding.

So, considering the overarching Jewish perspective, the book of Job does nothing less than question the very character of God. However, the purpose of Job "cannot be reduced to a single simple statement. The author seems to have a multifaceted purpose under the general theme of wisdom teaching about God and human suffering."[64] (See "Key Scriptures and Themes" below for a breakdown of each section's purpose). In the book of Job, we get to personally witness a grappling match between the relationship of a good, all-powerful Creator versus His allowance of intense human suffering. Considering the suffering He allows, what is He *really* like and how does that affect human life?

"Is God worth serving?" is another way to ask the big question of Job. In Job's dealing with this question, we must understand that it was not wrong or profane for him to ask questions. He asked in reverence as a true sufferer of pain simply seeking honest answers.

From the onset the author informs the reader that sin or judgment was not the cause of Job's situation. The opening verse of the book states: "In the land of Uz there lived a man whose name was Job. This man was blameless and upright; he feared God and shunned evil." Many more times through the book we are reminded of his uprightness before God even in his intense questioning. We are reminded of this immediately following

---

[64] Ibid., 858.

Satan's first attack as Job responded by falling to the ground in worship saying: "'Naked I came from my mother's womb, and naked I will depart. The Lord gave and the Lord has taken away; may the name of the Lord be praised.' In all this Job did not sin by charging God with wrongdoing" (Job 1:21–22).

Job's questions to God were not viewed by God as sin!

Key Scripture(s) and Theme(s)

Four main Themes run through the book of Job:

1. God allows the faithful to be tested (Job 1–2).
2. God allows His reputation to be put on trial (Job 3–37).
3. God answers the faithful, albeit not exactly in the manner we expect (Job 38–42:6).
4. –God vindicates those who remain faithful (Job 42:7–17).[65]

Contemporary Application

The book of Job gives us permission to do that which seems almost blasphemous—Job gives us biblical authority to *put God on trial*. Is the One True God worth serving? How does He contain all the love and power to prevent evil but still allows it? This is a very *deep* and *extremely personal* question, but it *is* OK to ask the question.

Some folks in the church-world today state we should never question God. And in some sense, they are correct. Our questions must be asked with the correct motive and attitude. Job questioned God very seriously but bathed those questions in total submission, obedience, and humility toward God (1:20–22, 2:10, 7:20, 9:3–4, 9:14–15, 9:32–35, 13:20–25, 16:15–17, 19:25–27, 21:16, 21:22, 23:1–7, 27:1–6, 31:5–8, 40:3–5, 42:1–17). And because of this, he was identified *very intentionally* in the opening verse as a blameless man. We must approach God with the same level of respect. The author wanted us to know that even the most faithful follower of God has questions that are perfectly OK to ask! After all, God knows our thoughts and feelings! We might as well be honest and respectfully approach Him in our quest for relief and answers.

---

[65] For more detail on these four points, see Paul R. House, *Old Testament Theology* (Downers Grove, IL: Intervarsity Press, 1998.), 428–38.

In this quest for relief, we can turn to the book of Job as it helps us understand the biblical reason for suffering. Eugene Merrill states it like this:

> Job provides the biblical answer to the problem of theodicy. God can work all things—even evil things—together for good (Romans 8:28), and those who are faithful to him to the end will benefit from the evil they must suffer. But this answer in Job is incomplete without the rest of biblical revelation. For it is in Jesus Christ that the greatest evils the world can offer—betrayal and crucifixion—meet with the ultimate good—forgiveness and cleansing.[66]

Reflecting on this is *not* for the faint of heart. It deals with the very question that has caused more people to walk away from God than probably all other issues combined. The philosophical line of thought goes like this: If God is all-powerful and all-loving, how can evil exist in the world? Why do we suffer so much if God has the power to change it and the love in His heart to do so? We experience so much unjustified pain in life so either God is not all-powerful or not all-loving. Which one? Do you see the quandary we're in? This is the very question posed by the highest-level critics to Christian philosophers and theologians.

Luckily, from a philosophical and theological standpoint, this question is considered answered by most. Our response to the problem of evil is called "theodicy." This is the term we use that describes our defense of how a good and all-powerful God allows evil. This term explains how God can allow us to suffer so much in this life.

So much has been said by so many authors on the topic of theodicy that we couldn't even begin to list all those that have contributed. However, a good start in your research journey would be to look at St. Augustine's writings on the free-will defense. Also, other older sources from church history on this topic are Thomas Aquinas and Francis of Assisi. This will start you down a good path from those older sources in church history. For

---

[66] Bill T. Arnold and Bryan E. Beyer, *Encountering Biblical Studies, Encountering the Old Testament*, ed. Eugene H. Merrill (Grand Rapids, MI: Baker Book House, 1999), 301.

more modern contributors, look at *The Problem of Pain* by C. S. Lewis, *Can God Be Trusted* by Graham Maxwell, Peter Kreeft's contributions, and Alvin Plantinga, just to name a few. Please understand this list is very brief and many other great God-fearing men and women have tackled this topic from several angles.

While the purpose of this book is not to outline an in-depth answer to why we suffer, we do want to apply the book of Job into our lives correctly. One thing to certainly keep in mind is that "Job indicates that wise living under extreme conditions is dependent upon divine revelation."[67] In other words, Job would have continued to be bitter had God not stepped in and revealed Himself in the end. And so it is with you and I—we wouldn't make it through many of the harsh realities of life without God's intervention.

Ultimately, God shines through as free and clear of all indictments brought against Him in Job. So now the question is: Will God be free and clear of all indictments brought against Him by you? He certainly proved Himself to be a good, loving God while allowing Job's trials, and He is also the same during ours.

I pray that you and I do not experience the same level of pain as did Job. Even so, we will certainly face the same questions at some level. When those questions arise, we can learn from the book of Job that *God can be trusted in spite of tragedy.*

---

[67] Paul R. House, *Old Testament Theology* (Downers Grove, IL: Intervarsity Press, 1998.), 524.

Psalms

Big Idea

Let us focus on God's greatness through worship and praise!

Author

While David wrote many of the Psalms, the entire book itself was authored by several people over the course of almost one thousand years and compiled by an editor sometime after the Babylonian Exile of the sixth century BC.

That being said, David is credited with writing seventy-three psalms. Asaph, according to 1 Chronicles 15–16, was King David's worship leader and is credited with writing twelve of the psalms (50, 73–83). The sons of Korah are attributed with psalms 44 and 85. Psalm 90 was credited to Moses while psalm 72 and 127 were written by Solomon. This leaves us with sixty psalms whose authorship is unknown but still provide us with wondrous descriptions of God and His ways.[68]

Original Recipients

The book of Psalms, as we have it now, was completed sometime after the Babylonian captivity was over, about five hundred years after King David's reign. Therefore, the original audience of its final form were postexilic Jews. However, the psalms as we have them today were initially five different writings that were circulated among God's people long before they were compiled into one book during the postexilic period. So the original audience spans a period of over five hundred years beginning with the reign of David (1,000 BC +/-) to after the release from the Babylonian exile in the early 500s BC.

Date of Writing

David lived, reigned, and wrote his portion of the psalms right around 1,000 BC, but many of the other psalms were written hundreds of years

---

[68] Bill T. Arnold and Bryan E. Beyer, *Encountering Biblical Studies, Encountering the Old Testament*, ed. Eugene H. Merrill (Grand Rapids, MI: Baker Book House, 1999), 304–5.

after David's death. It wasn't until after release from Babylonian captivity in 538 BCE that someone compiled them in their current form.

Historical Setting/Timeline of Events

Each individual psalm has its own distinct historical setting—some of them we're unaware of, but for most of them we have a solid or at least a decent understanding of the circumstances within which they were written. Some psalms we must simply read for what they are, but others are accompanied by a historical setting that serves to tremendously widen and deepen the breadth and beauty of God in our minds. From the mountaintop of praise to the valley of retreat … from the heights of success to the deepest pits of sinful regret … joy to hate, pain to pleasure … throughout the entire gamut of human emotion and experience we see the psalmist reaching for God with intensity and intentionality.

Main Characters

Our wonderful, indescribable, uncontainable, unimaginable, glorious, and Holy God is undoubtedly the main character of the psalms. In it He is described from so many different perspectives and vantage points. With each interaction with Him through the psalms we are introduced to an even greater and mightier God than previously understood.

We experience our wonderful God through the psalms as we see Him through the situations, environments, and perspectives of the authors. For example, King David is a main character in many psalms simply because he wrote them. They were birthed from situations he was in at the moment. Some of his psalms express David's worship of our great God (Psalm 8). Other psalms show David's heart as he was repenting from sin (Psalm 38, 51).

Purpose

When we read the psalms in English, we're receiving a translated version of 150 songs/poems that describe God from many different moods and perspectives. However, when it is read in its original Hebrew, so much more color and vibrance instantly spring forth. God inspired the authors to use many poetic literary techniques to eloquently and mesmerizingly portray an awesome God! Just like our worship songs today contain rhyme and rhythm, so too do the psalms in their original Hebrew.

Furthermore, the psalms teach that God's protection, leadership, guidance, discipline, and love for humanity never changes. Regardless of where we are in the gamut of human emotions, God is always there. In this book we see the pendulum of human emotion swing from deep pain, regret, and repentance to overwhelming joy, security, and trust in God. In contrast, we see God standing strong and steady as the majestic King. We see Him unwaveringly provide green pastures for His sheep to lie in even when life's deep valleys of death loom on the horizon.

Therefore, as a part of scripture's wisdom literature, the purpose of the psalms is to teach, instruct, inspire, and guide God's people to live lives filled with Godly wisdom. The psalmists were inspired to do this with the use of poetry and song as they worshipped God.

Key Scripture(s) and Theme(s)

Psalm 1 is the psalm upon which all other psalms hinge.

Study it. Memorize it. Breathe it. Live it. When you've accomplished that … study it. Memorize it. Breathe it. Live it again.

In addition to Psalm 1 being the hinge of the book, we also have divisions that separate the psalms into five distinct parts. The five divisions are chapters 1–41, 42–72, 73–89, 90–106, and 107–150. "The closing verses of the last psalm in each collection typically contain some kind of doxology or ascription of praise to the Lord that serves to 'tie off' that part of the Book of Psalms. The one exception is Psalm 150, a grand psalm of praise, that fittingly concludes the entire collection."[69]

In addition to the five divisions contained within the psalms, a German scholar Hermann Gunkel laid a solid foundation upon which most scholars have based their classification of genres found within the psalms. Based on Gunkel's work, Bill T. Arnold and Bryan E. Beyer have settled on seven genres that help in proper understanding. These genres

---

[69] Bill T. Arnold and Bryan E. Beyer, *Encountering Biblical Studies, Encountering the Old Testament*, ed. Eugene H. Merrill (Grand Rapids, MI: Baker Book House, 1999), 306.

are: hymns of praise, penitential psalms, wisdom psalms, royal psalms, messianic psalms, imprecatory psalms, and lament psalms.[70]

Hymns of praise—these psalms focus on praising God for who He is and what He has done. They contain some of the most beautiful descriptions of God's glory found in all scripture. These psalms provide wisdom by teaching God's people why and how to worship. Examples are Psalm 8, 136, and 150.

Penitential psalms—Penitential psalms are simply expressions of deep sorrow for sin. The psalmist was saying: "I repent. I apologize to you, Lord." The beautiful use of poetical expression to demonstrate the need for repentance provides a context for us all to feel comfortable admitting our failures. These psalms provide wisdom by teaching God's people that repentance is necessary and provide an outline for how to go about approaching God with our sin. Examples include Psalm 38 and 51.

Wisdom psalms—these psalms focus on general observations about life. By making observations about those who follow God and those who do not, the psalmist makes clear the end result of personal choices. Psalm 1 is a great example as it makes a general statement regarding how God intends life: "Blessed is the one who does not walk in step with the wicked ... Not so the wicked! ... for the Lord watches over the way of the righteous but the way of the wicked leads to destruction." These psalms provide wisdom by teaching that those who follow God will win, and those who do not follow God will lose. Whether in this life or the next, the righteous prevail, and the wicked perish. Other examples are Psalm 14 and 73.

Royal psalms—these psalms focus on the king of Israel, each emphasizing different aspects of the kingship. They provide wisdom by focusing on the king as God's special instrument at that point of God's "salvation history." They show how God was leading His people through history preparing and protecting them as they were the lineage through which He would bring about the Messiah. In other words, they teach that God was deeply involved not just with the coming of Jesus Christ but also in each century leading up to that very special moment. Examples of royal psalms are Psalm 2, 45, and 110.

Messianic psalms—The messianic psalms describe the Messiah and His coming. In tender eloquence and stout faith, the psalmist beautifully

---

[70] Ibid., 307–12.

depicts the salvation and hope that would come about when the long-awaited Messiah would arrive. Even though Psalm 2 is classified as a royal psalm above, it is also a messianic psalm and is quoted as such in the New Testament. Other examples are Psalm 16 and 22.

Imprecatory psalms—These psalms have caused debate among scholars in that they call on God to bring about judgment to the psalmist's enemies. One of them, Psalm 137, was written by an exile just after being overtaken by Babylon. This psalm portrays infant brutality as it calls for the Babylonian infants to be bashed against the rocks. However, the idea in these psalms is that the psalmist is turning to God in a time of dire need. A matter of life and death was before the psalmist on some occasions, and God was the only way of escape. The main way these psalms teach us wisdom is by giving us permission to be respectfully honest with God. Even though God doesn't always do what is asked of us to our enemies (i.e., bash their babies against the rocks), He still listens to us in every situation. The imprecatory psalms teach that God is big enough for us to be honest with Him. And because of that, He is worthy of our worship.

Lament psalms—Lament psalms typically come in a three-part form. First the psalmist cries out to God because of his circumstance. Next, the psalmist exclaims his faith and trust in God, and then ends with the third part, praise. Psalm 3 is a great example when David was king and yet found himself running from his son Absalom.

Contemporary Application

Willem A. VanGemeren sums up the twenty-first century application of the book of Psalms quite perfectly in his contribution to the *Expositor's Bible Commentary*. He states:

> The Book of Psalms is God's prescription for a complacent church, because through it he reveals how great, wonderful, magnificent, wise, and utterly awe-inspiring He is! If God's people before the Incarnation could have such a faith in the Lord, witnessing to his greatness and readiness to help, how much more should this be true among twentieth-century Christians! The Book of Psalms can revolutionize our devotional life, our family patterns,

and the fellowship and the witness of the church of Jesus Christ.[71]

We could quite simply leave it at that and have quite a summation of how we're to apply it into our lives, but let's dig in for a bit longer on what these psalms really look like lived out in our lives today.

First, have you ever been sad? The psalms are here for you. Are you struggling with sin? There are also psalms for you in that arena too. Are you dealing with anger toward those that have wronged you? David had quite a bit to say about that. Are you basking in the overwhelming presence and protection of God? Do you just want to thank Him for it? There are certainly psalms for you in that area as well!

No matter what emotion you're feeling, the psalmist has been there. And by digging into the psalms that apply to your specific situation, you can be better equipped to navigate through and grapple with the realities of life. Traversing through the mountaintops of joy, happiness, and success as well as the valleys of sadness, sorrow, and failure—the psalms will be with you through the entire journey of life.

Furthermore, and possibly more importantly, the psalms give us a prescription of how to handle the circumstances that bring about our emotions. In other words, the psalmist doesn't just deal with how you and I feel; he also addresses the cause of those feelings. Take for instance the famous Psalm 51—David sinned by committing adultery and then murder to cover it up! The woman he committed adultery with, Bathsheba, became pregnant, and as a part of David's punishment, the baby died shortly after birth. However, prior to the dreadful death of his child, he spent agonizing moments in deep prayer asking God to save the child. However, upon hearing the news of his baby boy's death, he washed himself and praised God! People thought he was crazy! But the lesson is this: when we've been under discipline from God our only choice is to worship Him. If David could do it in the context of losing a newborn, then you and I can also praise God as He brings us through repentance and discipline.

Ultimately, the psalms teach us that our God is indescribable—every description we can imagine is incompetent at portraying the reality of our

---

[71] Willem A. VanGemeren, "Psalms," In *The Expositor's Bible Commentary*, vol. 5, ed. Frank E. Gaebelein (Grand Rapids, MI: Zondervan, 1991), 5.

great, merciful, wonderful, beautiful, strong, ferocious, and loving Creator. Whatever you're dealing with, He's standing there steady … even as you waiver. This is why we can say the Big Idea of Psalms is: *Let us focus on God's greatness through worship and praise!*

Proverbs

Big Idea
Walking in godly wisdom is the way to win in this world.

Author
Solomon. The opening verse tells us "the proverbs of Solomon the son of David, king of Israel." Even if he didn't personally coin each proverb, he was king at the time of compilation and is credited for the book as we have it today.

Original Recipients
The nation of Israel during the time of King Solomon who ruled from 970 to 931 BC.

Date of Writing
The book was written and/or compiled during the reign of King Solomon from approximately 970–931 BC.

Historical Setting/Timeline of Events
Solomon ruled the great nation of Israel from his father David's death in 970 BCE to his own death in approximately 931 BC. During this time, Solomon made several observations of the nation and its people. He saw many wise, honorable, and good actions that led to a life blessed by God. He also witnessed unwise, foolish, and ill-advised decisions that led to disaster. From these observations of the nation and its people, King Solomon determined what it meant to flesh out godly wisdom. He was able to provide us a written standard for that which makes God smile versus that which makes Him frown.

The result of his observational efforts is the book of Proverbs.

Main Characters
God is the main character in the book of Proverbs. This book is not written in story form like other books of the Bible. Therefore, traditional main characters, plots, and storylines do not exist. However, the book

of Proverbs continually centers the reader's focus back to God and godly wisdom.

Purpose

When we fail to view the book of Proverbs through the lens of Jewish understanding, we simply fail to understand it as it was intended. The Jewish canon categorizes Job, Ecclesiastes, and Proverbs to be the only books contained within the wisdom literature genre while we as Christians add Psalms and Song of Songs. *Please* reread the subsection "Wisdom Literature According to Jewish Tradition" in the introduction to wisdom literature for a clearer understanding before moving on.

That being said, Paul House summarizes the purpose of Proverbs quite simply as he states: "Proverbs is definitely a manual for appropriate living under God's leadership."[72]

Key Scripture(s) and Theme(s)

The key scripture in Proverbs is found in the opening of chapter 1. Here, Solomon gives the purpose of the book as "to know wisdom and instruction." In other words, Solomon was saying "read this if you want to be wise," but he concludes by saying, "the fear of the Lord is the beginning of knowledge, but fools despise wisdom and instruction." In essence, Solomon was conveying that we are to lead lives in the fear of the Lord because no one can be wise without knowing God.

In addition to the opening key verses, Proverbs can also be separated into three distinct parts that each provide their own angle of gaining godly wisdom. Part 1 consists of Proverbs 1–9 and introduces God as He calls *everyone* to pursue His wisdom. Part 2 entails chapters 10–24 and uses Solomon's sayings to teach how the righteous should act throughout many specific situations of life. And the third section consists of chapters 25–31 as they focus on how God desires leaders to act.[73]

---

[72] Paul R. House, *Old Testament Theology* (Downers Grove, IL: Intervarsity Press, 1998.), 441. House was summarizing Crawford Toy's thought in Crawford Howell Toy, *A critical and Exegetical Commentary on the Book of Proverbs*, International Critical Commentaries (New York: Scribner's, 1904), 10–16.

[73] Paul R. House, *Old Testament Theology* (Downers Grove, IL: Intervarsity Press, 1998), 441.

Contemporary Application

Do you want to know what it means to be full of godly wisdom? Do you want to know what it takes to navigate through this fallen world in a manner pleasing to the Lord? Do you feel as if you would better yourself by gaining wisdom for God? If you answered yes to any of these questions, then the book of Proverbs is for you.

Containing short sayings as well as longer expositions of prose and poetry, this book was inspired by God and given to us through the wisest man that ever lived. Covering topics from sexual purity to wise decision-making, it is the apex source for gaining God's wisdom. Through the Proverbs, we gain proficiency and prowess in living for Him in an ungodly world.

When reading Proverbs, I usually stick to just a few short sayings each day to give me something I can chew on. I simply take the one, two, or three sayings and focus on how to apply them in my given circumstances of the day. For instance, Proverbs 18:12 states: "Before a downfall the heart is haughty, but humility comes before honor." This is something I can directly apply to just about any circumstance as I make an intentional attempt to practice being humble instead of being arrogant. I certainly don't know everything, so there's quite a reason for me to be humble. Another example is Proverbs 10:17. It says: "Whoever heeds discipline shows the way to life, but whoever ignores correction leads others astray." We all make mistakes in life and sometimes need corrective action brought into our lives. The fool becomes upset at correction, but the wise gladly welcomes it. So, when discipline comes my way, I need to listen to it, learn from it and ensure the same mistake isn't repeated. Humbly accepting correction is the godly standard when we find ourselves in error.

So much practical godly wisdom can be learned from the Proverbs. When applied, it can radically transform us and confirm that *walking in godly wisdom is the way to win in this world.*

Be blessed, friend.

Ecclesiastes

Big Idea

Life is meaningless without the Lord.

Author

Ultimately, we do not know who wrote Ecclesiastes. Upon reading the introduction, it appears that Solomon was the author, but that has been widely debated by scholars for many reasons. For our purposes, we will simply state that we are unsure. Regardless of the earthly author, we can rest assure that the wisdom contained therein can only come from God.

Original Recipients

Although the Israelites were the original recipients, we're not certain of which generation. Therefore, all we can say is that the original audience was the ancient Israelites, sometime between the reign of King Solomon (971–931 BC) and the Babylonian captivity (586 BC).

Date of Writing

Some scholars date the writing after the exile of the fifth century BCE, but this has recently been mostly discredited based upon the differences between the writing styles and word choices of the pre-exilic and postexilic periods.[74] Likely it was written during the preexilic period, and very possibly in the lifetime of Solomon, which would give us a date in the tenth century (900s) BCE. For our purposes we will stick to a date of writing in the lifetime of Solomon, though this position must be taken humbly.

Historical Setting/Timeline of Events

Based on the information above under the heading "Date of Writing," we are not certain of the historical setting. However, with this specific book, the historical setting is not nearly as important to understanding its message as it is in other books.

---

[74] Daniel C. Fredericks, *Qoheleth's Language: Re-evaluating Its Nature and Date* (Lewiston, NY: Mellen, 1988), 266–78.

Main Characters

Ecclesiastes is written from the perspective of the *Qoheleth*, or *teacher* in most modern translations. This is not a traditional story but more so a memoir of the Qoheleth as he was on a quest for the purpose of life. Ultimately, he could not ascertain the full and complete purpose of humanity based upon any level of human experience or intellect. Therefore, he was forced to rely on God and simply follow Him *even though it didn't always make sense from a human perspective.*

Purpose

When we fail to view the book of Ecclesiastes through the lens of Jewish understanding, we simply fail to understand it as it was intended. The Jewish canon categorizes Job, Ecclesiastes, and Proverbs to be the only books contained within the "wisdom literature" genre while we Christians have added Psalms and Song of Songs to our categorization. *Please* reread the subsection "Wisdom Literature According to Jewish Tradition" in the introduction to wisdom literature for a clearer understanding prior to continuing.

Considering the Jewish perspective, the Qoheleth, or teacher in Ecclesiastes, expressed much frustration with the words translated in the NIV "Meaningless! Meaningless! Everything is meaningless!" In the Hebrew this word is *hebel* and can be translated as frustrated, meaningless, absurd, etc. To the Hebrew mind, it painted a word-picture of a vapor that is here one second and gone the next. In other words, the reason the Qoheleth was so frustrated was because he knew that no matter how successful he was in life, everything he accomplished and even he himself would all eventually disappear as quickly as a vapor.

Death is inevitable no matter what, but even though there is a definite dark tone to the book, the message is very clear: nothing permanent can ever be accomplished in this physical world. Consequently, a life outside the permanence of God is absurd and meaningless. God must be the center of thought, goals, actions, and accomplishments, or existence is meaningless regardless of how successful one may become.

Key Scripture(s) and Theme(s)

Anytime you see a word or phrase repeatedly used in scripture, you can automatically know it is very important. Ecclesiastes is a perfect example where thirty-eight times we see the phrase (or a variant of it) "Meaningless! Meaningless! Says the teacher. Everything is meaningless!" So it is here at this juncture that we must pause for a bit to unpack this phrase if we are to best understand God's message contained in this book.

In the case with Ecclesiastes, this phrase "Meaningless! Meaningless!" must be viewed through the lens of the ending of the book. The last two verses of the book (12:13–14) really wrap up the point very nicely for us as they state: "Now all has been heard; here is the conclusion of the matter: Fear God and keep His commandments, for this is the whole duty of man. For God will bring every deed into judgment, including every hidden thing, whether it is good or evil." In other words, much like the book of Job, God is telling us in Ecclesiastes *that some things are simply above our paygrade.* Yet, we're called to serve Him in faith, trust, and obedience even though the "big picture" hasn't been revealed to us. Anything outside of fearing God and keeping His commands is meaningless because it falls outside the spectrum of His will as determined by the "big picture" we've not been educated about.

Contemporary Application

This one is quite simple: our lives are without purpose, without meaning, and utterly pointless if we do not follow the Creator of the universe, Jesus Christ. Period. End of story. This reality is most definitely not an easy grappling partner. Yet it is certainly true, and when properly accepted, it will lead you to being quite the grappler yourself.

But why is everything meaningless outside of following God even when we don't understand the "why" behind all His directives? Sometimes His ways just simply do not make sense! If you've ever felt this way, you're not alone! But let's look at it this way: we must humbly admit that God has certainly not revealed *everything* to us. He has only revealed to us, in His Word, that which we need to know to gain an eternity into His presence. But He hasn't told us *everything*—that's why we have so many questions about life, meaning, purpose, etc.!

Unquestionably there is more going on out there than we know about.

And somehow we are playing a successful part in his great plan when we "fear God and keep his commandments." But we fail at playing that part when we turn away from Him.

We don't and can't understand the entirety of His purpose. All we can do as a human race is serve as one little cog in the wheel. For there is, as scripture tells us, far more out there that is too great for us to comprehend. So we must simply trust Him.

Listen, the point is very simple. One day I am going to die. Period. And to further darken the story, if I'm like most of humanity, my name will not be remembered even within my own family after about four or five generations. Ever thought of it like that? Pause with me and think about it this way: do you know your great-great-grandfather's and great-great-grandmother's name? Most of us do not. That's only four generations ago, and they aren't even remembered by their own descendants. That puts it into perspective and teaches me that maybe what I've got going on in this life that seems so important *to me* really isn't all that great. Unless … unless I invest my few short days on Earth into a much greater and larger cause—the cause of Christ. In this manner, no matter how short my life may be, its meaning will be compounded throughout time like a ripple in water. The work will continue after my death. And this is the only way to find meaning and purpose.

Regardless of our accomplishments toward what *we* individually consider to be important, we will never find fulfillment unless we submit those goals and accomplishments to God. We each have different priorities in life and place importance on very different lifestyles. We individuals define "a life committed to a good cause" in extremely different and subjective ways. We all have very different opinions on causes that are good enough to dedicate our lives to following. The key to finding happiness and fulfillment in those causes, careers, goals, or ambitions is to have a mind that is daily submitted to God. I personally find a peaceful and relaxing contentment when my daily routine is bathed in thoughts on God. On the contrary, I become very grumbly and irritably dissatisfied with even the best of times when my mind wanders away from Him. Ecclesiastes confirms why we feel this way: Life is *meaningless* without the Lord.

God has created us to feel discontented when we stray from Him. It is simply one of the gauges He has placed in our lives that we are to use to perform self-assessments regarding our relationship with Him.

Remember, in the end everything in this physical world goes away. Therefore, do not fall in love with this world and that which it has to offer. It is only temporary, and you will die soon anyway, so it doesn't matter. Focus on God and His plan. Throw yourself into His plan. Abandon your own will, goals, pleasures, desires, ambitions, and whatever it is that *you* consider to be important in life. Abandoning those temporary and finite causes allows us to join the permanent and infinite cause of Christ. For outside that, everything is meaningless—*life is meaningless without the Lord.*

The freedom that comes from living in the truth that you are not the center of yourself is unexplainably liberating. I hope you experience it, my friend. I am currently learning to experience this myself.

Song of Songs

Big Idea
God has blessed us with the blissfulness of biblical marriage.

Author
Chapter 1 verse 1 simply opens with "Solomon's song of songs." This could mean it was written by him, but it could also mean that the author lived during the time of Solomon's reign or dedicated the songs to him. Regardless, traditional scholarship deems Solomon the author, and we'll stick with that safe bet. Even if we're incorrect, the meaning and application of the book doesn't change.

Original Recipients
If Solomon or one of his contemporaries wrote it, the original audience would have been the nation of Israel during Solomon's rule (971–931 BC) or shortly thereafter.

Date of Writing
Given our assumption that Solomon is the author, it's safe to say it was written after he began reigning as king. So we'll stick with a date of writing somewhere within his reign from 971–931 BCE, a little less than one thousand years before Christ.

Historical Setting/Timeline of Events
Solomon, who served as king of God's people from 971–931 BC, spent considerable time observing the kingdom and its individuals. This observation inspired him to pen the wisdom contained within the Proverbs. It only makes sense that through his general observations, he also assembled the ability to recognize that which makes up a good marriage … and a bad marriage. It is this reflection on the joys of young love and lasting marriages that served as inspiration for the Song of Songs.

Main Characters
The main characters are a beautiful bride and a handsome groom as they celebrate the joys of a godly marriage.

Purpose

Song of Songs is an ancient Near Eastern anthology of wedding songs. Individually, the songs were likely used in weddings and then gathered later in the current form we have today, much like the Psalms. Song of Songs displays a beautiful depiction of married love in six episodes. Each episode begins by depicting courtship between a man and a woman, followed by the wedding, then consummation and their life together. Closure is brought to each episode as the friends of the bride and groom are addressed.

Key Scripture(s) and Theme(s)

While we won't be trying to determine a key scripture in the Song of Songs, we can certainly look at the major theme rolling through the pages of the Song of Songs. Running right next to the Big Idea, the main theme of the book is simply that marriage and sexuality can be an incredible source of joy if they are experienced as God intended.

Contemporary Application

Israel was surrounded by pagan nations that worshipped false gods. As a part of the pagan worship of these nations, individuals were encouraged to have sexual relations in their temples ... with temple prostitutes ... out in the open. The pagan belief was that the gods would look down on the sexual acts, become sexually aroused, and fertilize the ground with rain. This rain served as fertilization to the ground and their crops much like a man fertilizes a woman through the sexual act. How twisted a perspective on human sexuality!?

While our culture today doesn't practice sexuality as described above, we all know that our secular society is burdened by a misguided and misaligned perspective. Today we simply do what we want, and we justify it by any means necessary. We want it *our* way, and we want it *now*. This is embedded so deeply in our secular culture that I personally believe that if we thought temple prostitution would cause food to grow, we would find a way to legalize it.

In contrast, we find interwoven through this book such beautiful purity with regard to biblical marriage and sexuality. The tapestry of romantic love is celebrated, encouraged, and praised within marriage. A handsome groom, his beautiful bride, and the joys they express as they follow God in their marriage is something to truly admire. It is here, in the holy scriptures, that you find the joy and beauty of marriage and human sexuality as intended by the One True God. The delights of married love and real biblical sexuality are a part of God's Creation and *He has declared it very good.*

The Song of Songs gives you permission to enjoy the *unbridled beauty* of the marriage bed with your husband or wife. Listen, as much as our culture has opened the market on sexuality and abused it with labels of atrocity, God *created* it and called it good. So let us couple the Song of Songs with the rest of scripture discussing marriage and sexuality and enjoy the great harvest of rewards with which God intended to bless His people.

I pray you allow God to bless your marriage and your sexuality. He created both, and He has called them good. Celebrate, enjoy, and feel no shame as you pursue biblical marriage and biblical sexuality.

CHAPTER 9

Prophets

One of the most misunderstood genres of literature in the Bible is prophecy—and for good reason. Typically, these books don't open with any background information or significant explanation of historical context. Some of them open with who served as king during the prophecy, but we're not really given much more than that. However, what may appear to be absent-minded omission to us fifteen hundred to nineteen hundred years later actually made perfect sense to the original recipients of the prophecies. The situations and cultures of the original recipients was the historical context of the prophets' writings, so there was no need to outline in detail why the prophet was writing. In other words, each prophecy was written about people, to those people, so they already understood the context within which they were living. They did not need to have their own surroundings and circumstances explained to them like we do because they were there ... and we were not.

For those who are well versed in ancient and biblical history, the prophets do in fact allude to their historical circumstances in quite a direct fashion. They do this by mentioning not only who was king but also situations, events, and circumstances. However, most of us do not generally catch on to the historical context within which the prophets wrote unless we also study biblical history. Still, we cannot lose sight of the fact that while we may have a tough time understanding the message of the prophets, they remain unbelievably applicable to us today! So our job becomes one of finding the meaning of each prophet by first being able to place the prophet's words within a context or setting. The only authentic way to do this is to look at biblical texts outside the prophets as well as extrabiblical writings to piece together and discover the canvas upon which to cast the words we read.

So, let's briefly outline a "big-picture" historical context of the prophets so we can better drop them into their setting as we read and study them.

As we begin this journey, we need to understand that the glory days of David and Solomon (1010–970, 970–931 BC, respectively) were long gone. After Solomon died, the unified kingdom was split into the northern kingdom of Israel and the southern kingdom of Judah. At this point the brother nations fell into deep spiritual and economic ruin. The accountability they previously had due to great godly leadership died with David and Solomon. So they rebelled against God ... and this is where the prophets step in. God brought the prophets onto the scene of this tragedy to convince them to avoid the consequences of their sin, which was death.

So where do we look in the Bible to locate the historical setting of the prophets? Well, many folks correctly assume the prophets are the last main characters of the Old Testament simply because they are the last books contained therein. This is *kind of* true. What many people do not realize is that the prophets take place within the historical setting of the previously discussed genre of historical books. Yes, that is right—each Old Testament prophet can be dropped down into the context and storyline of the historical books, mainly 1 and 2 Kings as well as 1 and 2 Chronicles. (If you've skipped the historical books, it would be best to at least read the introduction in the previous pages before moving further into the prophets).

To continue this thought regarding historical context, it is extremely beneficial for us to go back even further than David and Solomon. As part of understanding the context of any given prophet, we must understand not only what was going on with God's people during the time of the prophet but also the events that led up to needing prophets in the first place. So, let's trek back to before David and Solomon ... let's briefly go back to the beginning.

God put Adam and Eve in the garden. Shortly thereafter, they disobeyed so God spared them by sending them out of the garden so they would not eat from the Tree of Life and live forever in their sinful state. (What a blessing in disguise!) Sometime later, we humans became so evil that God sent a flood to kill everyone except Noah and his family (Genesis 6–9). God started over, but we humans repopulated and once again became evil. This time, instead of starting over, God decided it was time to move on to the next phase of His plan to save us from ourselves. This was where God declared Abraham (Genesis 12) and his lineage to be the vehicle through which He would one day bring about the Messiah. (The story of Abraham likely took place about 2,300 years BC.)

Centuries passed, and Abraham's many descendants found themselves in Egyptian slavery (Exodus 1). This was where Moses came onto the scene in the fifteenth century BC (date is debatable) and led Israel out of slavery. Unfortunately, due to Moses's disobedience, he was not allowed to enter the Promised Land. Joshua took the reins around 1405 BC and led Israel throughout their campaigns as they conquered the land God had given them. Shortly thereafter, around 1385–1380 BC, the people began turning their backs on God, so He began sending other nations to overtake and oppress them. This was His rod of discipline so Israel would turn back to Him. The tactic worked, and each time Israel would repent, God would raise up a judge, more like a military leader, who would lead Israel in driving out their enemies and regaining their freedom. This happened twelve times with twelve different judges, one from each tribe of Israel, over the course of about two thousand years (1385–1185 BC, approximately). Finally, upset and fearful of the threats of the surrounding nations, Israel stood in defiance to God's plan and demanded a king (1 Samuel 8). King Saul started off well but failed miserably, which led to the tremendous successes of King David (1010–970 BC) followed by his son King Solomon (970–931 BC).

When King Solomon died approximately 931 BC, the nation of Israel was divided into the northern kingdom of Israel and the southern kingdom of Judah. This is the tragic point that marked the beginning of the unending downward spiral of spiritual decline and the eroding of that which had been previously built. It was during this time that the level of godliness and true religion was on a sharp decline as both nations allowed Canaanite idolatry to pervade. In addition, the social injustices transacted among God's people as well as the perversion of sexuality had spread like a virus.

Through all this, God never gave up on His people—so during this era He sent His prophets. The prophets were an attempt to call His people back to Him, as well as to encourage them after they had undergone His discipline. So, when we read the Old Testament prophets, we're reading the writings of "those individuals who live from about 800 BC to 450 BC and served as God's special messengers to his people by the power of the Holy Spirit."[75] The prophets were sent in an attempt by God to steer His people away from the cliff toward which they were heading full steam.

Even though God spoke clearly through His prophets, most of the era of the kings was spent in rebellion to Him. As a matter of fact, the northern kingdom of Israel never held a godly king, which ultimately led to its permanent downfall in 722–721 BC. Second Kings 17 records this tragic scenario where God used Assyria to take them into captivity as discipline.

The northern kingdom never recovered.

A little over a century later, the southern kingdom of Judah was also taken into captivity in 605 BC by the Babylonians, ultimately culminating with the destruction of the temple in 586 BC (2 Kings 24–25). However, unlike the northern kingdom, God did not allow Judah to be completely lost. For it was within the nation of Judah that we find the lineage of David tucked away and quietly marching throughout history. And it is this very lineage that would continue to relentlessly rally throughout time to one day bring about the Messiah, regardless of their catastrophic failures. No matter the external and internal battles of God's people, God's plan to save all humanity would not fail! This was *promised* to Abraham, and God was not about to break his side of the covenant regardless of humanity's failures!

A final note to keep in mind before we conclude: Our tendency to view the prophets as some sort of mystic voice foretelling future events is somewhat justified. Yet, in reality, the prophets spent far more time simply addressing the people in their contemporary setting much like our preachers do today. Yes, they foretold the future, but they spent far more time dealing with the people's present situations to lead them back to God.

---

[75] Bill T. Arnold and Bryan E. Beyer, *Encountering Biblical Studies, Encountering the Old Testament*, ed. Eugene H. Merrill (Grand Rapids, MI: Baker Book House, 1999), 341.

Mark J. Boda explains this idea in his contribution to the *NIV Application Commentary*:

Although this aspect of prophetic ministry must be celebrated, a perusal of the prophetic books as well as the New Testament provides a fuller picture. The prophets do, it is true, speak of future events, the "foretelling" aspect of prophetic ministry, but most of their prophecies were focused on the values and actions of their contemporaries, the "forthtelling" aspect of prophetic ministry. Even when they spoke of future events, in nearly every case they did so with an eye on the present generation. The prophets were also concerned with the past. They often recited the story of Israel (both its positive and negative elements) to challenge the present generation to obedience (see Jeremiah 2; Ezekiel 16, 18, 20; Hosea 11).[76]

In conclusion, when you read what appears to be "gloom and doom," please remember that it is always *redemptive in purpose* as illustrated by almost every prophet ending their book with a promise of restoration. God was trying to steer His people back into the purpose to which He called them. Just like an engine is created to operate within a certain RPM range, they too were created to be His vehicle that operated in a certain manner. This vehicle's job was to properly make the trek throughout history, one day arriving at the destination of the Messiah. They could do this *only* if they operated within the safe RPM ranges provided by God.

They were not created to withstand the high RPM and subsequent pressures that manifested as the worship of false gods, mistreatment of one another, and the practice of perverted sexuality. So, God was trying to guide them back to the safe and secure "RPM range" within which the vehicle of salvation could eventually arrive at the Messiah. This was accomplished through the prophets as they served as the RPM gauge. But when His people ignored the gauge, God turned to the pagan nations of Assyria, Babylon, and Persia to serve as the onboard computer to shut down the engine just prior to total engine failure.

God succeeded.

We now have our Messiah.

His name is Jesus Christ.

Thank you, Lord.

---

[76] Mark J. Boda, "Haggai, Zechariah," in *NIV Application Commentary*, ed. Terry C. Muck (Grand Rapids, MI: Zondervan, 2004), 36.

Isaiah

Big Idea
Discipline equals deliverance! Repentance equals restoration!

Author
Isaiah, son of Amoz (Isaiah 1:1).

Original Recipients
Isaiah originally prophesied to the southern kingdom of Judah for about forty years. This began approximately 740 BCE when King Uzziah died and ended around 700 BCE[77] during the Assyrian siege of Jerusalem.

Date of Writing
"The composition of Isaiah may be placed sometime after 701 BC and before the prophet's death."[78] This was about two hundred years after King Solomon's death and the dividing of the kingdom into Israel and Judah (931 BC) but during the fall of Israel in 721 BC and about 100 to 150 years prior to the fall of Judah in 605–586 BC.

This has been debated, though, as some claim there is considerable evidence that much of it was written or at least compiled later during the Babylonian captivity that began in 605 BC.[79]

Historical Setting/Timeline of Events
The ruthless powerhouse of Assyria was ransacking the globe in the eighth century BC, dominating and conquering all in her path. The northern kingdom of Israel found themselves staring down the barrel of the fierce Assyrian army and crumbled to their authority. Their sins had finally drawn down the wrath of God as He used this mighty Assyria as His rod of discipline.

Judah observed ...

---

[77] Robert B. Hughes And J. Carl Laney, *Tyndale Concise Bible Commentary* (Wheaton, IL: Tyndale House, 1990), 253.

[78] Ibid., 253.

[79] Marvin A. Sweeney, "The Latter Prophets," in *The Hebrew Bible Today: An Introduction to Critical Issues*, eds. Steven L. McKenzie and Matt Patrick Graham (Louisville, KY: Westminster John Knox Press, 1998), 75–76.

Judah observed their brothers fall as they were taken into captivity for their sins. They must have thought: *Are we next?*

It was just prior to and after this Assyrian Crisis with Israel that Isaiah addressed Judah and highly recommended that she repent, which worked for a time. As Judah watched her brothers fall to Assyria, they showed themselves friendly to Babylon. God interpreted this as a clear indication that Judah sought to trust in human alliances versus trusting in Him. Upon being confronted by Isaiah for reaching out to Babylon (2 Kings 20:12–19), Hezekiah and Judah repented and avoided the reach of the great Assyrian empire. However, Isaiah prophesied to Judah's king Hezekiah that the very nation in which they attempted to place their trust would be the nation to whom they would be made subjects. This is the message of Isaiah chapters 1–39. Yet, Isaiah also expounded greatly in prophesying a recovery period and restoration of the people in the final chapters (40–66).

Main Characters

Isaiah, a handful of kings, and the southern kingdom of Judah.

Purpose

The southern kingdom of Judah was treacherously traveling the trail of treason. They had, in many ways, forsaken God by turning to idolatry and social injustices. God called Isaiah to lead them into repentance and back into their purpose of delivering the lineage of Christ from one Testament to the other.

We would completely miss the entire purpose of Isaiah if we did not pull into the discussion the forecast Isaiah provided of the Messiah. While the first half of Isaiah focuses on judgment, with a bit of hope peppered throughout, the second half specifically fleshes out the reason for the hope the people were to have, despite the coming judgment. This is where we find the famous passages like that of Isaiah 53 speaking directly about the Messiah.

Just as the original recipients of Isaiah were to soon go through a period of humiliation before they rose to victory, so too, the Messiah would enter the world in a humble manner. He would endure the greatest of humiliation right alongside them before taking His throne as Creator and Ruler of the entire cosmos.

One passage that captures this concept perfectly is found in chapter 6. This chapter opens with: "In the year that King Uzziah died, I saw the Lord, high and exalted, seated on a throne; and the train of His robe filled the temple." On one hand, the nation of Judah had a dead king. On the other hand, they had a very shaky world scene with the most powerful nation at the time circling them looking for someone to conquer. Certainly, the people were in a panic! What were they to do? Well, Isaiah 6 reminded them who was really in control. While their earthly king was dead, the One True King of the entire cosmos was alive and well!

Isaiah 6 exclaims that He was high and exalted on His throne! But then we see a strange phrase immediately following claiming that the train of His robe filled the temple. Now, on its surface, you and I may not understand what this means, but to the people of Isaiah's day the message was clear! His train represented His presence … and it filled the entire temple! In modern terms, Isaiah said that while their earthly king was dead, the true King was alive and well! His presence was everywhere! His authority was absolute! No need to panic—He's got this under control … His Messiah was coming!

And this Messiah would start with very humble beginnings only later to endure excruciating humiliation just like they were about to endure. In essence, this Messiah was about to sit down in the mud of life with them *only to lift them out of it.*

Key Scripture(s) and Theme(s)

The book, as briefly addressed above, consists of two sections. Section one contains chapters 1–39, which is comprised of three subsections that each warn of God's judgment due to Jerusalem's idolatry and the mistreatment of one another. Ultimately these warnings end with the prediction of the fall of Jerusalem to Babylon, found in chapter 39.

Chapters 40–66 make up the second section and focus on the *future* restoration and hope for God's people. This total and complete shift in purpose has led some scholars to believe the second section was written by someone else a few centuries later. However, from the conservative approach we are taking, we discard that hypothesis. The shift in thought and message is strictly due to Isaiah's forward thinking of restoration and the hope that the latter part of the book intended to convey—as opposed to the direct warnings of the first half.[80]

As previously stated, we would be remiss if the Messiah wasn't brought up as a major theme of Isaiah. Ultimately, the second half of Isaiah, the half that addresses restoration and hope, does so with the Messiah at center stage. This is confirmed several times in the New Testament as it refers to and quotes from Isaiah to confirm the validity of Jesus Christ.

Contemporary Application

Sometimes we must endure the discipline of our loving Lord because, well, quite frankly, we really know how to mess things up. But please allow me to remind you that when we undergo God's discipline, we can rest assured it means He hasn't given up on us.

Isaiah prophesied that the entire nation of Judah would soon be led into captivity (God's discipline) for two reasons: idolatry and social injustices.

1. Idolatry. This may look a little different in our lives than it did in the life of Judah, but it's still all the same. We should take heed to this call of repentance and turn away from anything that we put before God. As a matter of fact, if anything is even remotely close to God on our "scale of importance," we should part ways with it. I don't mean abandon your family, of course, but certainly the point has been made that nothing is to be placed above God. Is it your career, your prestige, your goals, your toys? If so, get rid of them immediately! He cannot and will not tolerate idolatry in our lives. We know it when we see it.

2. Social injustice. This one is an absolute epidemic in our modern society. Much like idolatry, you know it when you see it. The nation of Judah was judged for mistreating one another. The rich were oppressing the poor and punishing the innocent (to name a few). Listen, corruption and money can get you just about anywhere you want to go in this life, but it leads to only one place in the next life. Period. Whether it's mishandling facts about

---

[80] Robert B. Hughes and J. Carl Laney, *Tyndale Concise Bible Commentary* (Wheaton, IL: Tyndale House, 1990), 253.

someone else to get the promotion at work or utilizing a sneaky loophole to take from the poor, just stop. Isaiah says to just stop. Social injustice can be anything from radical and clearly visible fraud on a multimillion-dollar level all the way to one individual simply taking advantage of another through deceit or greed.

In the end, chapters 1–39 teach us to serve God only and serve our fellow humans by treating them as you would like to be treated.

Moving to a much brighter note, chapters 40–66 teach us that there is always hope! The people of Judah had not yet experienced the coming of the Messiah, but we have! We know the full story! We have the end of the book. And even though our Savior appeared for the first time in a humble manner and endured extreme humiliation by dying on a cross, we cannot forget that He also rose from the dead! The authority required to raise oneself from the dead should be the guarantee in our hearts that He will do what He said He will do!

He came the first time as a humble servant, but He is coming the second time in all His splendor and might! And when that day comes, Revelation tells us, His enemies will march out in battle against Him, cause a big scene, beat their chests, raise their swords, and shout the battle cry. But when Jesus Christ steps out, He will simply speak, and the battle will be over!

It was His very word that spoke everything into existence, and it will be His very word that will speak all evil out of existence!

So take heart and know that when we as individuals or as a nation undergo God's discipline, He is showing us that He hasn't given up. His plan will never fail! This is why we can stand firm on the Big Idea of Isaiah:

Discipline equals deliverance! Repentance equals restoration!

Be blessed. Take courage. The prophecies in Isaiah about the first coming of our Messiah came true. This adds to our firm confidence that the remaining prophecies throughout the Bible about His Second Coming will also come true!

Jeremiah

Big Idea
The *plan* of God prevails over people's peril.

Author
Jeremiah the prophet, as he dictated to his secretary, Baruch.

Original Recipients
Jeremiah originally prophesied to the southern kingdom of Judah for about forty years under the reigns of King Josiah (640–609 BC), Jehoiakim (609–597 BC), and Zedekiah (597–586 BC). In essence, he prophesied up to the Babylonian captivity culminating in 586 BCE with the destruction of the temple.

Date of Writing
According to Jeremiah 1:2, God first called Jeremiah to prophesy in the thirteenth year of Josiah's reign, which would give us a start date for his ministry of 627 BCE (see "Original Recipients" for Josiah's reign). "Jeremiah had prophesied for twenty years before God told him to write his messages down,"[81] so the math tells us he first began writing his messages about 607 BCE.

Historical Setting/Timeline of Events
The events in this book took place from 627–586 BCE.[82] The northern kingdom of Israel had long fallen to the Assyrians a century prior in 721 BCE. Now, at this point, the three powerhouses on the world scene (Egypt, Assyria, and Babylon) were all vying for the dominant position. Two big battles between Babylon and Egypt, one is 609 BCE and the other in 605 BCE, resulted in Babylon assuming the right to call themselves the new world power. Even with Assyria siding with Egypt in the 605 BCE battle, they couldn't stand against fierce newcomer Babylon. During this same time frame, and shortly thereafter, the people of God in the southern

---

[81] Robert B. Hughes and J. Carl Laney, *Tyndale Concise Bible Commentary* (Wheaton, IL: Tyndale House, 1990), 272.
[82] Ibid., 271.

kingdom of Judah were also in the crosshairs of the Babylonian army. They knew they couldn't overcome—they knew they too would fall. And fall they did.

For a parallel reading, start in 2 Kings 24 for the historical books' record of the Babylonian captivity.

Main Characters

Jeremiah, Judah's kings Josiah, Jehoiakim, and Zedekiah, and the nation of Babylon.

Purpose

The people of God had been carried off into exile by Babylon. Was it because the One True God was weak? Was it because He had abandoned His people? Absolutely not. To counteract any false suppositions as to their circumstances, "the book was designed to show the exiles the reasons for their captivity."[83] God had not grown weary, tired, weak, or forgetful. He certainly did not abandon His covenant. God called the prophet Jeremiah to prophesy to Judah so they could be certain that they were in captivity because of their unfaithfulness to God. However, as is the case with most prophetic books of the Old Testament, Jeremiah also encouraged them to endure the seventy years of exile. Restoration and freedom was indeed their destiny, and Jeremiah confirmed this with the people of Judah.

Key Scripture(s) and Theme(s)

Jeremiah 1–29 and 34–52 focus on the reality that Judah lost everything because of their unfaithfulness to God. It's here that we find the infamous Jeremiah 29:11 as it states: "For I know the plans I have for you, plans to prosper you and not to harm you, plans to give you a hope and a future." This phrase was originally uttered to Judah as she was marching into captivity. God was communicating that they were going into captivity as discipline because they had been unfaithful to Him. Yet, they were to understand that even while under His rod of discipline, God still had a plan for them ... a good plan ... a plan for success.

In contrast to the previous sections discussed, chapters 30–33 outline the promise of God to restore them under a new covenant from which

---

[83] Ibid., 271.

Ezekiel

Big Idea
Returning to God from rebellion results in restoration and reward.

Author
Ezekiel 1:3 states that Ezekiel the priest, the son of Buzi, was the author.

Original Recipients
The original recipients were the exiled people of Jerusalem as they were under Babylonian captivity in the sixth century BCE.

Date of Writing
As can be seen below in the "Historical Setting/Timeline of Events," Ezekiel served as a prophet for about twenty-two years beginning on his thirtieth birthday in 592 BCE. It's most likely that Ezekiel penned his prophesies during or shortly after he first announced them to the people of God in the sixth century BCE.

Historical Setting/Timeline of Events
The year is 597 BCE. The Babylonian exile of Judah had already begun (see 2 Kings 24:8–17), and Ezekiel found himself being carried off as one of the exiles. Alongside him were several other high-ranking officials such as King Jehoiachin, the nobles, priests, and other influential people of Judah. The sins of the people had finally come crashing down on them, just as prophesied by Isaiah (2 Kings 20:16–18) and Jeremiah.

Five years later, in 592 BCE, the book of Ezekiel opens with the man Ezekiel sitting on the banks of the Kebar River, in exile. It was his thirtieth birthday. This birthday would have been very celebratory if the captivity had never taken place and he was back in his homeland. His thirtieth birthday was supposed to be his induction into the priesthood but, instead, he sat lonely on the banks of a foreign river.

But as he sat there a subordinate to a foreign pagan nation, the Lord had not forgotten him. It was in this lonely moment that instead of being inducted into the priesthood, the Lord established him as a prophet!

This would continue for about twenty-two years until about 570 BCE. Ezekiel, then, instead of serving as a priest in the temple, was called to be a "watcher over the exiled nation of Israel, and was in this capacity to *continue* the work of the earlier prophets, especially that of Jeremiah, with whom he in several ways associates himself in his prophecies; to preach to his contemporaries the judgment and salvation of God, to convert them to the Lord their God."[85] In essence, God still used Ezekiel in a very special way, just like his contemporary Jeremiah, to serve Him and His people. Yet, unlike another one of his contemporaries, Daniel, the prophet Ezekiel would live and die in captivity never to see with his own eyes the closure of the exile.

For a parallel reading, start in 2 Kings 24 for the historical books' record of the Babylonian exile.

Main Characters

The main characters are Ezekiel as the prophet, Judah as the unfaithful children to God, and Babylon as God's hand of discipline toward His people.

Purpose[86]

Ezekiel was called as a prophet to watch over those who were alongside him in Babylonian captivity. But even more importantly, God called him to answer the question "Why has our God allowed this pagan nation to overtake us and carry us off into captivity?" One commentator wraps up this concept by stating: "The task that was assigned to Ezekiel was to prophesy to the exiles of Judah, who had been carried away into captivity in distant Babylonia. It was an audience close to despair, asking why this disaster had come on them and where God was in the middle of their personal holocaust."[87] Ezekiel provided an answer the people did not want to hear. As a matter of fact, God told Ezekiel that his message would be

---

[85] C. F. Keil and F. Delitzsch, *Commentary on the Old Testament,* vol. 9: Ezekiel, Daniel. By C. F. Keil. Translated by James Martin and M. G. Easton. (Peabody: Hendrickson, 1996), 1.

[86] This entire section was influenced by theBibleProject.com.

[87] Iain M. Duguid, "Ezekiel," In *The NIV Application Commentary,* ed. Terry Muck (Grand Rapids, MI: Zondervan, 1999), 35.

ignored (Ezekiel 3:7). But Ezekiel also provided hope as He clearly told the story of how God would restore them to the original garden state found in Genesis.

We can demonstrate this purpose best by dividing Ezekiel into two main sections that can each be divided even further into subdivisions, each with their own contribution to the Big Idea and purpose.

1. Chapters 1–33: "Your sins are your downfall."
    a. Chapters 1–11 answer the question "Why are we in exile?" It does this by stating that it was their own sin, rebellion, and unfaithfulness to God. Their blatant rebellion was so bad that God had abandoned the temple, as shown in Ezekiel's first vision, to allow it to be destroyed. However, chapter 11 also gave them hope of restoration that will be further expounded upon in later sections of this book.
    b. Chapters 12–24 announce the judgments on Judah for their sin by comparing Jerusalem to a burnt stick in chapter 15, a rebellious wife in chapter 16, a dangerous but captured lion in chapter 17, and two promiscuous sisters in chapter 18. Certainly, the judgments against them were well-deserved. Even if Noah, Daniel, and Job were crying out to God, Ezekiel says, it would still be too late. The gavel of cosmic authority had been dropped.
    c. Chapters 25–32 announce God's judgments on the rest of the world. Philistia, Edom, Moab, and Ammon were all geographically close to Jerusalem and were judged for their contribution to Jerusalem's sins. God then moved on to judge the two most powerful nations in the area: Egypt and Tyre. They had grown extremely prideful and considered themselves as gods. They simply could not hold themselves up against God's justice.
    d. Chapter 33 wraps this up with a short story told to Ezekiel by a refugee who had just arrived from Jerusalem. But this wasn't just any short story ... this was news that Jerusalem had been destroyed along with the temple. Ezekiel's prophetic warnings had been ignored, and the inevitable had finally happened.

2. Chapters 34–48 "Restoration is for *all* nations and all creation."

    a. Chapters 34–37 promise a "new David" and a "new people." God was going to replace their hard hearts with soft hearts. This is demonstrated through the vision of the valley of dry bones. These dry bones were a metaphor for Jerusalem's spiritual state. But God was going to send His Spirit and breathe fresh life into them, resulting in skin and flesh reappearing to bring life. This is all a reflection back to the Creation when God took dirt and breathed upon it to create humankind. But now evil was so engrained into humanity's heart that a "new creation" was necessary.

    b. Chapters 38–39 answer the question: "What about all the other nations?" This is where God promised to root out *all* evil from *all* nations. Even the evilest nations, represented by Gog and Magog, would have new hearts! Gog is shown as destroyed four separate times in these chapters. This solidified the fact that God would certainly end all evil with a finality that could not be overturned. And then He would replace it with a people of pure hearts toward Him.

    c. Chapters 40–46 outline how once all evil was eradicated, the greatest temple would be established forever. Hope would be restored, all evil gone—only God's presence blanketing the people. Sounds a lot like what God was going to do almost six hundred years later in the life of Jesus Christ. And it sounds a lot like a place Genesis calls The Garden—the same place referred to in Revelation as the New Heaven and the New Earth! Ezekiel, at the end of his book, gives a description of this garden and called it "The Lord Is There" (46:35). It is here that we see so much imagery from the Garden of Eden, a place to which we all can return, a place where God's presence will reign in our hearts and in our lives.

In the book of Ezekiel we see God's intent was always to be inclusive of all humanity with His salvation. Hope was given to God's people because of the harsh yet restorative book of Ezekiel.

Key Scripture(s) and Theme(s)

So many passages and oracles represent the concept of judgment on God's people for their sins, but Ezekiel 5:8–9 will suffice for our purposes: "Therefore this is what the Sovereign Lord says: I myself am against you, Jerusalem, and I will inflict punishment on you in the sight of the nations. Because of all your detestable idols, I will do to you what I have never done before and will never do again."

The garden to which we all return one day if we follow God is given its title in the last words of the book: "The Lord Is There." This is such a beautiful description of the wonderful garden state from which we were removed in Genesis. Thankfully, God worked so patiently with us throughout the entire Bible, bringing us back to it in Revelation. Isn't that really what the Bible is after all—the story of God saving us from ourselves?

Ezekiel 36:26 really sums up the heart of the Big Idea of Ezekiel: "I will give you a new heart and put a new spirit in you; I will remove from you your heart of stone and give you a heart of flesh." This is truly the message of Ezekiel.

Contemporary Application

There are two very clear applications for us in the book of Ezekiel: (1) God will not and cannot tolerate our sin, and (2) God has provided a way for us to obtain a new heart, one that is soft toward Him.

First, our sin. Sin is so confined these days to a list of dos and don'ts, but it is so much more than that. The New Testament defines sin as "missing the mark," an archery term used when someone didn't hit the bullseye. Anytime we do anything that misses the bullseye, even just a little bit, it is sin—even if it moves us just a slight distance from that perfect score. But why does God require a perfect score? For us to be able to mingle with God, who is perfect, we too must be perfect. It really is quite that simple. And though our actions will never be 100 percent perfect, our heart and spirit can be made perfect by the way provided through Christ. Otherwise, our imperfect state cannot mix with His perfect nature.

To illustrate this: you cannot mix red and white paint and maintain the characteristics of both. In the same way, you cannot mix the perfection of God and the imperfection of humankind and maintain the character of both. God cannot, by definition, mix with imperfection. If He could, He would no longer be perfect. This is why He has chosen to give us the hope of the latter part of Ezekiel and make us perfect one day.

It is this very hope that leads us to the second significant application from Ezekiel: God will one day annihilate all evil and usher in a new era like that which was present before the fall! In the story of the valley of dry bones we see imagery clearly referencing the creation. In the Genesis account of creation, God mixed dirt and His breath to give life. But we turned against Him, so Ezekiel teaches that He is going to do the same thing all over again! This is the whole message contained in the dry bones story. Ultimately it is the message contained in the whole book of Ezekiel! One day our hard hearts will be swapped for soft ones!

Looking back into New Testament history, a luxury Ezekiel didn't have, we can see the full picture of the process God was in during the exile of Ezekiel's day. We now have the cold, hard facts of exactly how God breathed life back into our dead bones! Let this be an encouragement to you that God's plan worked through Jesus Christ! The first Adam messed it up, but a second Adam, Jesus Christ, came and unmade the mess! This is why returning to God from rebellion results in restoration and reward!

We simply cannot be with God one day if we choose to continue in the ways of the first Adam. But if we walk in the way of the second Adam, Jesus Christ, we will one day be made perfect and brought back to that original garden state referenced at the end of the book of Ezekiel.

In essence, when you find Jesus, you find the hope proclaimed in Ezekiel.

Daniel

Big Idea

The One True God has no rival, period.

Author

Daniel is the author as we see chapter 8 open with the words "I Daniel …" Jesus even confirms this in the New Testament as He states in Matthew 24:15 "So when you see standing in the holy place 'the abomination that causes desolation,' spoken of through the prophet Daniel …." However, debate in the last few centuries has brought into question whether some sort of editor later compiled the current version we read today. See "Date of Writing" for more detail.

Original Recipients

The southern kingdom of Judah had been ransacked and led off into exile, causing them to question their faith. This book was originally written to them.

Date of Writing

The events of Daniel took place sometime during the Babylonian captivity in the sixth century BCE after the temple was destroyed in 586 BCE. Traditionally it has been believed that the book was also written during this time by a noble named Daniel, one of the captives. While we certainly know that Daniel provided the first person accounts in the last six chapters, there has been considerable discussion as to if some sort of editor(s) later in the second century BCE compiled the book into the version we read today. Regardless, we know that Daniel lived during the Babylonian exile as one of the captives in the sixth century BCE, which is when the book was originated.[88]

A note to remember regarding the authorship and date of writing: in light of the questions in recent scholarship, the message, purpose, and application of the book into our lives remains the same. Theological value

---

[88] See the Introduction to Wendy L. Widder, "Daniel," In *The Story of God Bible Commentary*, eds. Tremper Longman III and Scot McKnight (Grand Rapids, MI: Zondervan, 2016) for a detailed conversation on the issue of authorship and date.

doesn't change, so please do not let these conversations and debates distract you from the truth contained therein. Jesus Himself stated that Daniel was a prophet, but that doesn't mean that Daniel had to personally write every word for it to be inspired of God. Daniel could have certainly written the first account and then passed it on to others who edited, expounded, and rearranged the text. Either way, the entire process was directed and guided by God Himself. Wendy Widder summarized this view quite nicely as she says: "Thus, the position of this commentary is that the accounts in the book of Daniel reflect events that happened to a real Daniel and his Judean peers in sixth-century BC-Babylonian exile, and that the prophecies are accurate. However, the question of who ultimately compiled the book, what editorial work they might have done in it, and when that happened cannot be definitely answered."[89] (This also applies to several other books in the Bible as well).

Historical Setting/Timeline of Events

Daniel, his close associates, and the southern kingdom of Judah had been conquered, overrun, and carried off into exile by the great and mighty force called Babylon. This event alone, taking place in 605 BCE, was bad enough as it basically sent a shock wave throughout the entire world claiming the Babylonian gods were superior to the One True God. But to make matters worse, some years later in 586 BCE, the Babylonians went so far as to destroy the temple in Jerusalem, ultimately cementing in the minds of many of the faithful that their hope in God was futile. The situation was dire; hope was dwindling, and the people of God needed a reminder of who they served—the One True Almighty God to whom against no one or no god could stand.

Main Characters

Daniel, Shadrach, Meshach, and Abednego.

Purpose

"The message of the book of Daniel is that, just as the God of Israel saved Daniel and his friends from their enemies, so he would save all Israel

---

[89] Wendy L. Widder, "Daniel," In *The Story of God Bible Commentary*, eds. Tremper Longman III and Scot McKnight (Grand Rapids, MI: Zondervan, 2016), 5.

in their present oppression."[90] In the minds of Daniel's contemporaries, everything they believed regarding the power and might of the One True God was crushed before their eyes. They had been carried off into captivity, and their temple to God was destroyed. From their perspective, and according to the mindset of the *world* at the time, the fact that Babylon came in and destroyed God's temple was a clear indictment that the pagan gods were more powerful than God Himself. This was the message the world, at that time, understood to be absolute truth.

The book of Daniel was written to God's people to clear up this falsity. Daniel's message was that God has no rival, and this will not be doubted by anyone … in any country … or throughout any period. The book of Daniel is an example of a man digging deep and trusting in the One True God regardless of his circumstances. He definitively communicated that when God finally decided to step in and end the childish games being played by the Babylonians, no one would doubt the power of the One True God.

Key Scripture(s) and Theme(s)

The book of Daniel is separated neatly into two evenly divided sections. The first six chapters are a narrative description of Daniel, Shadrach, Meshach, and Abednego. This section expounds on their experiences in Babylonian captivity. The last six chapters are apocalyptic prophecies regarding their future. (It is very interesting to note and is worth the time for you to personally study how this affects their placement in the Jewish Bible versus the Christian Bible. The Jewish Bible seems to place the significance on the first six chapters by placing the book into its narrative genre while the Christian Bible focuses on its prophecy by placing it among the prophets).

Daniel 6:26–28 serves as the key scripture and was ironically issued as a decree to all of Babylon by Darius their king after Daniel was saved from the lion's den:

"'For He is the living God and He endures forever; His kingdom will not be destroyed, His dominion will never end. He rescues and He saves; He performs signs and wonders in the heavens and on the earth. He has

---

[90] Mark Zvi Brettler, *How to Read The Bible* (Philadelphia: Jewish Publication Society, 2005), 218.

rescued Daniel from the power of the lions.' So Daniel prospered during the reign of Darius and the reign of Cyrus the Persian."

I say the pagan king Darius summarized it quite nicely, don't you think?

Contemporary Application

God has no rival. No one or nothing even comes close.

All God's enemies fall somewhere within the framework of His creation, so it is safe to say that no one created by Him can stand against Him.

So my question to you is this: If God wins no matter what, and if you've chosen to be on His side, who also wins? You do. It *is* that simple, even though our circumstances sometimes provide evidence otherwise.

Daniel was actually thrown into the lion's den ...

The three Hebrew children were actually thrown into the fiery furnace ...

They held true and won. This should drive you with an unparalleled passion to do the same regardless of the circumstances that make up your bone-crushing fiery situation. God wins. Period. Stand with Him, and you also get to win. It really is that simple, even when it truly seems and feels otherwise.

I'm certainly not trying to minimize your hurts, bumps, bruises, and calamities in this life. I'm just stating that considering God's glory and the glory that awaits us, the biggest of issues in our lives today will appear as simple inconveniences once we're in His presence. So, while we should always remain sensitive to one another's atrocities, we can still join hands with Daniel and encourage one another with the reality that God has no rival! We all win in the end if we draw our swords and march into battle alongside God and not against Him!

This is so important to understand in light of the reality that "the book of Daniel is often read for its contribution to our understanding of end-times events, but sometimes Christians have been so obsessed with this that we have missed its main message: God is in control, no matter how things look, and his kingdom will one day fill the earth."[91] So even if it appears that you lose in this life ... even if you're on your death bed and

---

[91] Wendy L. Widder, "Daniel," In *The Story of God Bible Commentary*, eds. Tremper Longman III and Scot McKnight (Grand Rapids, MI: Zondervan, 2016), 5.

it seems that a "Loss" will be placed next to your name when you pass on, you must remember that it is simply not true. Those who stand with the One that has no rival will still be standing once the battle is over. Period.

Stay strong. Walk as one full of grit—the grit required to win. For even in what appears to be loss, we win when we stick to the One True God. This was true in the life of Daniel, as well as with his associates and the nation of Judah. Therefore, it will be true of you and I as well. Stay strong. Maintain hope. For the One True God has no rival, period.

Hosea

Big Idea

The right ways of God restore the righteous and ruin the rebellious.

Author

Hosea, son of Beeri (Hosea 1:1).

Original Recipients

Hosea was originally written to the northern kingdom of Israel, just before their fall to Assyria in 721 BCE. Though the southern kingdom of Judah is briefly mentioned, the prophecy is mostly directed at Israel.

Date of Writing

Hosea's ministry lasted from at least 753 BCE to 715 BCE but he makes no mention of the fall to Assyria in 722–721 BCE. Therefore, his writing was likely completed prior to then. So, we're looking at a date of writing sometime between 753 and 722–721 BCE.[92]

Historical Setting/Timeline of Events

The glory days of Kings David and Solomon (1010–931 BCE) were long gone. God's people were no longer considered a world power. Assyria was dominating the world and was beginning to align its sights on the northern kingdom of Israel. It was during this period in the mid700s BCE that Israel had a very serious choice to make—a choice that would have grave and permanent consequences.

Main Characters

The main characters are Hosea, his adulterous wife Gomer, the rebellious nation of Israel (the northern kingdom after the split in 931 BCE), and a loving God desiring reunification with His people.

---

[92] Leon J. Wood, "Hosea," In *The Expositor's Bible Commentary,* vol. 7, ed. Frank E. Gaebelein (Grand Rapids, MI: Zondervan, 1985), 161–63.

Purpose

The point of no return was looming over Israel like a dark raincloud. They had utterly abandoned God and had turned to the false gods of the surrounding nations. At this point, God had already spent about two centuries reaching out to His people through the prophets. But the nation simply would not listen. As a final attempt, He used Hosea to serve as His prophet in a very strange and radical way.

God called Hosea to take back his adulterous wife as an expression of (1) how Israel had become adulterous toward God, and (2) how God was willing to take back His disloyal people, the northern kingdom of Israel. Unfortunately, they did not listen, so God used Assyria to take them into captivity in 722–721 BCE … a captivity from which they would never escape.

Key Scripture(s) and Theme(s)

Hosea 1:2 depicts how God viewed Israel's adultery toward Him as it states: "When the Lord began to speak through Hosea, the Lord said to him, 'Go, marry a promiscuous woman and have children with her, for like an adulterous wife this land is guilty of unfaithfulness to the Lord.'"

Hosea 14 speaks in great length of God's desire to see His people return to Him. It begins with "Return, Israel, to the Lord your God. Your sins have been your downfall!" It continues in verse 4 with, "I will heal their waywardness and love them freely, for my anger has turned away from them."

Finally, the single verse that summarizes the entirety of the book was penned as the last words of Hosea: "The ways of the Lord are right; the righteous walk in them, but the rebellious stumble in them." This is truly the epitome of God's message of love and repentance through Hosea. The Lord was communicating that He knew better and had their best interest in mind. He was beckoning them to follow Him and thrive, but they chose to ignore Him. They chose the quiet and dark path of disappearance from history.

Contemporary Application

The Assyrian captivity had most likely not yet taken place during the time the book of Hosea was penned. What this means for us is that we get a true glimpse into the heart of God as He makes a final attempt to call His people back to Him. When reading the prophets, many people simply see a "gloom and doom" message from God, almost as if He wants to harm folks or stifle their fun. This is not the case at all! We would be wise to understand that God used the prophets as a warning sign to call us back to safety. We were not created to withstand the kind of pressure we put ourselves through when we disobey God. When we sin or disobey, we're essentially preparing to jump from a cliff that we won't survive. The prophets, including Hosea, simply call us not to jump just like they did the original recipients. God's beckoning to you and I is out of love.

God has designed us to function at our maximum potential only within specific conditions. When we place ourselves outside those conditions we begin to degrade and wear, much like an engine revved beyond its intended maximum RPM. In contrast, we humans have been called by God to serve as the vehicle through which He brings salvation to our specific generation. When we choose not to operate with the RPM spec as designed by God, we cause the entire machine to suffer. God will not allow that.

The good thing is that the book of Hosea serves not only as a mirror to humanity's waywardness but also provides a reflection of how God seeks to restore us. Our heavenly Father's hands are wide open and welcoming our return. During the time of Hosea, God's people had become so indescribably corrupt, but He still called to them! If you've stepped out of His will, I urge you to return to Him before it's too late. Folks, we must remember that *the right ways of God restore the righteous and ruin the rebellious.*

Israel chose to continue running blindly in a direction that led to their death—despite God's outcry to return to Him.

They made their choice.

Now it's time to make ours.

Joel

Big Idea

External worship is legitimized by internal transformation.

Author

This book is named after its author, Joel, which means "Yahweh is God." We know very little about Joel, which also affects "Date of Writing" and "Historical Setting/Timeline of Events" below. Regardless, we know he was a great man of faith who served God wholeheartedly.

Original Recipients

The original recipient was the southern kingdom of Judah, most likely in the eighth century BCE. This was a time of economic prosperity under the reign of King Uzziah, the tenth king of Judah, who ruled from 792 to 740 BCE. Second Chronicles 26 outlines the accomplishments of King Uzziah. He started well by serving God but eventually allowed pride to creep in and bring about his ruin.

Date of Writing

Though the date of writing and historical setting are highly debated with considerable evidence for various positions, "the early eighth century BCE best harmonizes with the known data."[93]

Historical Setting/Timeline of Events

Assuming the original recipient was the southern kingdom of Judah in the eighth century BCE, the setting is one of economic prosperity but spiritual bankruptcy. King Uzziah had successfully led many military campaigns that led Judah into its most successful years, second only to that of the united kingdom under David and Solomon.

---

[93] Richard D. Patterson, "Joel," In *The Expositor's Bible Commentary, vol. 7*, ed. Frank E. Gaebelein (Grand Rapids, MI: Zondervan, 1985), 232.

Main Characters

While Joel plays an important prophetic role, the true main characters are: (1) the God of the cosmos as He tries to reconcile compassionately with His people, and (2) a complacent and stubborn Judah.

Purpose

Due to the successful military exploits and the resulting economic prosperity under King Uzziah, the southern kingdom of Judah had cozied up to their "self-made" comforts. They had forgotten who truly led them to success. God was the one who had blessed Judah and, as a result, they had taken Him for granted. Central to their depravity, Judah had allowed the sacrificial system and priestly duties to simply become an external formality while refusing to allow internal change. They looked good on the outside but were spiritually bankrupt on the inside.

The mentality of the day was "we are God's chosen people, and we are following the sacrificial formula, therefore He is *obligated* to bless us."

Judah was certainly God's chosen people. They were also following the temple regulations. Yet they were dead internally. God would not be forced to build His kingdom upon this hollow shell of spirituality. This is the central message of Joel.

To demonstrate this to His people, a devastating plague of locusts was sent that disrupted their economic success (1:4). This disruption was so great that it even impeded their ability to continue following the sacrificial system. God was halting their outward display of lies by interrupting their supply chain that provided resources to perform sacrifices. He was forcing their external condition to match their internal depravity. All the external obligations had to be a true representation of their internal condition, or He didn't want them.

Furthermore, God called Joel to articulate that even this great plague was nothing in comparison to the devastation that would come upon them if they continued to walk away from God.

Key Scripture(s) and Theme(s)

Joel 1:4 depicts the intensity with which the locust plague devastated the land, as a foretelling of what the foreign enemies would do if God's people did not repent. "What the locust swarm has left the great locusts have eaten; what the great locusts have left the young locusts have eaten; what the young locusts have left other locusts have eaten."

Joel 2:28 clearly articulates the point that God will restore His people from their waywardness: "And afterward, I will pour out my Spirit on all people. Your sons and daughters will prophesy, your old men will dream dreams, your young men will see visions."

Contemporary Application

A modern description of Judah's spirituality during Joel's time would be to say they went to church every Sunday but clearly did not live it Monday through Saturday. They were very careful to attend Wednesday night services, but their co-workers from earlier in the day would not be able to connect their church attendance with their daily lives. They did all the right external things on church days but internally they were simply without God.

Does this sound familiar? Specifically, does this sound familiar to *you* and *your* household? You see, most of us, me included, can quickly identify *others* who fall into this category. But the real question is, do *you* fall into this trap? At the end of time when you stand before God you will answer only for yourself. So, before we become quick to identify others' pitfalls, we would be wise to perform an honest self-audit of our own depravities. Before I can help others, I must first know and live the path myself.

Honestly, there have been many times when my internal spiritual temperature did not match my outward appearance of health. And I'm not speaking of years past. I'm speaking of current times. As a matter of fact, I'm quite good at struggling with inward rebellion while appearing to be in sync outwardly. Therefore, it is *my* duty to remain vigilant and place markers in my life that serve to give me a *measurable* contrast between my internal and external spiritual temperatures. Joel teaches me this. And Jesus reaffirmed it in Matthew 23:27–28 when he referred to the teachers of the law as "whitewashed tombs." They were pretty on the outside but full of dead men's bones on the inside.

One of the main measurable markers I personally use to discern where I am with God is how I treat my wife. If I'm not being a godly husband and treating Rebekah with utmost respect, I automatically know this is an indication that I need to step back and prepare for change in my heart.

A measurable marker of my personal spirituality is how I treat the lovely, beautiful, and graceful bride God has allowed me to serve. After all, God has called me to be the head of the household. So, if I'm not properly serving, protecting, providing for, cherishing, and making room for her to make mistakes, how can I expect God to do the same with me? This is real life application of the book of Joel. This is only one way I personally ensure my external spirituality is supported by my internal spirituality. For my external worship is legitimized only by my internal condition.

What are some ways you can ensure your external worship is legitimate? If it's not, you can be certain that God will deal with it one way or another. No one is exempt from His blessings … or His curses. So, it's best to deal with it now versus later. May God bless you and may your external worship be built upon the solid foundation of internal transformation. For *external worship is legitimized by internal transformation.*

Amos

Big Idea

To love God is to love people.

Author

This book was named after its author, Amos. Amos was a sheepherder in Judah but also tended sycamore trees to supplement his income.

Original Recipients

Though Amos belonged to the southern kingdom of Judah, he prophesied to the northern kingdom of Israel.

Date of Writing

Amos most likely prophesied and wrote sometime between 767 and 753 BCE.[94]

Historical Setting/Timeline of Events

Amos prophesied in tandem with Hosea to the northern kingdom of Israel during the reigns of Jeroboam II over Israel (793–753 BCE) and King Uzziah of Judah (792–739 BCE).

Main Characters

While several other nations are judged in the book of Amos, the northern kingdom of Israel is the focal point of the prophecy.

Purpose

Due to their economic prosperity, Israel had allowed spiritual rot and decay to pervade. Specifically, Amos addressed and condemned their sins of social injustice, exploitation of the poor, and sexual misconduct. But what makes this book unique is the *absurdly genius approach* used by Amos to lure Israel into condemning themselves!

And this is how he did it.

---

[94] Bill T. Arnold and Bryan E. Beyer, *Encountering Biblical Studies, Encountering the Old Testament*, ed. Eugene H. Merrill (Grand Rapids, MI: Baker Book House, 1999), 444–48. (Also serves as base for most information on Amos in this book).

Amos marched north from Judah and began prophesying to Israel for their mistreatment of humanity. However, instead of immediately addressing their sin, he started by condemning all of Israel's surrounding enemies for the same sins. First, he prophesied against Damascus, the northern enemy of Israel. At this point, you could almost hear the cheers of Israel as they swept across the nation. But swiftly, Amos swung the crosshair of judgment down to Gaza, another enemy of Israel residing to their southwest. Now you can imagine a true shout of victory emerging from the camp of Israel as enemies to their north and south are under fire from the Lord! But Amos didn't stop there. Next, Amos fired on the enemies of Israel living to their northwest in Tyre. And from Tyre he spun a quick 180-degree turn and fired on three more enemies of Israel: Edom, Ammon, and Moab. What started as cheers has now turned into a full-blown celebration in Israel. All their enemies were doomed!

Just as Israel thought their reason for celebration couldn't be any better, Amos turned both smoking barrels and fired on their hated brothers of Judah in the south. At this point, there could be no greater reason to celebrate in Israel! The excitement and festivity couldn't get any louder! Finally … their enemies including their arrogant brothers to the south in Judah were finally being brought low for their sins against humanity! They were finally being called into account for how they had mistreated, harmed, and slaughtered people. Their enemies were being called into account for their social injustices.

The smoke of rapid fire was so thick that Israel couldn't even see who the next victim would be. But the moment the smoke cleared just enough for them to barely gaze through the haze, they had a moment's notice to realize both barrels were aimed square at them.

Boom.

Boom.

Israel would fall for the same sins committed by their enemies. In rejoicing over the punishment of their enemies, they guaranteed their own demise. They were judged with the same judgment they cast upon their enemies.

The common belief of Israel at the time was that God had irrevocably committed to their success regardless of their lifestyle. The perspective of the day reflected something like this: "God made a covenant with us, therefore He *has to honor it.*" This perverted view and their lack of responsibly in handling God's covenant led to their downfall. They had clearly forgotten that they too were under obligation.

In Exodus 19:5 God's people had just come out of Egyptian slavery and were congregated at the foot of Mount Sinai. Here God made His covenant with them and said: *"Now if you obey me fully and keep my covenant, then* out of all nations you will be my treasured possession." But here in Amos several centuries later, they had forgotten God's covenant was always based upon an if/then statement. *If* they followed Him, *then* He would bless them."

They deceived themselves into believing that God would honor the covenant if they continued the religious rituals of sacrifice and temple worship. They thought wrong. God plainly communicated that their external worship was only valid if it was a true reflection of their inward heart.

Boom. Boom.

Key Scripture(s) and Theme(s)

Amos 2:6–8 records the judgment of Israel after they had celebrated due to the judgment of their enemies: It reads like this: "This is what the Lord says: 'For three sins of Israel, even for four, I will not relent. They sell the innocent for silver, and the needy for a pair of sandals. They trample on the heads of the poor as on the dust of the ground and deny justice to the oppressed. Father and son use the same girl and so profane my holy name. They lie down beside every altar on garments taken in pledge. In the house of their god they drink wine taken as fines." The three themes from these verses are as follows:

Theme 1: God accepts outward worship if it is legitimized by avoiding social injustice.

Theme 2: God accepts outward worship if it is legitimized by treating the needy properly.

Theme 3: God accepts outward worship if it is legitimized by godly sexuality.

Contemporary Application

We've all felt the sting of resentment as we observe the Sunday morning worship of an oppressive, shrewd, and immoral individual. The image of guilty individuals displaying themselves as innocent is a very unsettling experience. Furthermore, seeing these individuals get away with it is even more disturbing. But may the book of Amos serve as a reminder that God sees through all the fanfare. He knows the actions and inclinations of every heart.

Just as the nation of Israel was judged for their mistreatment of people and their rotten sexuality, we are held to the same standard today.

Think of it this way: a tree usually dies from the inside out. It can look healthy on the outside, sprouting green leaves in the spring, but internally, at its core, it has begun to decay and weaken. Eventually, a strong wind or storm will crash it to the ground. So goes it with us. We may look good on the outside but eventually our internal state will lead to our fall.

Considering this, please do not be dismayed when you see the guilty get away with their crimes toward humanity. Eventually, all things are brought into the light. When you see the poor oppressed, please do not lose heart. When you see the success of the immoral, please do not lose heart. For one day God will provide judgment and swift retribution for those that mistreat His people. Those who pervert the sexuality He deemed good will answer for their crimes.

But just as Amos turned the tides on the nation of Israel, the tides are now also turned on you. Are you that individual who creates a gut-wrenching resentment in the heart of others? Have others ever observed your outward worship and clearly viewed a disconnect from your inward character? Unfortunately, I have been that individual at times in my life. Thank the Lord Almighty for repentance and forgiveness. If you've ever been in the position I've been in, you have breached the covenant God made with you to save your soul. Please be careful and remember *to love God is to love people.*

Obadiah

Big Idea
You reap what you sow.

Author
The book bears the same name as its author, Obadiah. Nothing is told to us about Obadiah as an individual.

Original Recipients
The nation of Edom. The Edomites were descendants of Esau, which made them brothers to Judah.

Date of Writing
Though it has been debated among scholars, the most likely date this prophecy took place was sometime shortly after Jerusalem fell to Babylon[95] in 586 BCE.

Historical Setting/Timeline of Events
Obadiah is one of only a few books in the Bible that is a single chapter long. However, contained in this small book is a historical setting just as rich and deep as any other book. Edom had settled their land to the south and east of the Dead Sea all the way back as far as the patriarchal times of Abraham, Isaac, and Jacob. And still over one thousand years later during the time of King David (1,000 BCE +/-), hostility grew between them and God's people. If the date of writing above is correct, Jerusalem was overrun by the Babylonian nation, which likely received help from the Edomites.

Main Characters
Obadiah was prophesying to the main character of Edom.

---

[95] Bill T. Arnold and Bryan E. Beyer, *Encountering Biblical Studies, Encountering the Old Testament*, ed. Eugene H. Merrill (Grand Rapids, MI: Baker Book House, 1999), 452.

Purpose

This is one of only two Old Testament prophetic books that was directed solely at someone other than God's people. Though this prophecy centers on the destruction of Edom for their sinful dealings with Judah, the real point is the success of God as He leads His people. God will not allow the abuse of His people to go unabated regardless of the perpetrator.

The nation of Edom had committed great atrocities against their brother Judah. As a result, they would fall under the heavy hand and unquenchable wrath of God Almighty.

Key Scripture(s) and Theme(s)

Verses 10–12a serve as the key to understanding the book in its proper context: "Because of the violence against your brother Jacob, you will be covered with shame; you will be destroyed forever. On the day you stood aloof while strangers carried off his wealth and foreigners entered his gates and cast lots for Jerusalem, you were like one of them. You should not gloat over your brother in the day of his misfortune."

We also see their arrogance in verse 3: "The pride of your heart has deceived you, you who live in the clefts of the rocks and make your home on the heights, you who say to yourself, 'Who can bring me down to the ground?'"

Finally, the summarization of not only Edom's situation but also our contemporary application is found in verse 15: "The day of the Lord is near for all nations. As you have done, it will be done to you; your deeds will return upon your own head."

Contemporary Application

You reap what you sow—such a common phrase but penned so perfectly in the book of Obadiah. The nation of Edom sat directly on Judah's southeastern border providing them full view of their deadly actions toward God's people. And in their pride, God brought down the gavel on their intentional acts of disgrace and negligence. So often we are also blinded by our own pride and allow joy to creep in at the destruction of our enemies. But what if our enemies aren't the only bad guys? What if our enemies are friends of God? Everyone, except for the truly psychotic criminals, thinks they're the good guys in most altercations. But have you ever stopped to think about the bigger picture and which side you're really on?

The good news is that if you're reading this, you're probably trying your best to live for Him—you're probably on the good side. So, considering that when you go through a rough patch where God is disciplining you, rest easy when your foe gloats over your pain. Rest easy when those around you seem to "hit a man while he's down." Shake off the unnecessary judgment of your fellow humans and know that God doesn't condemn; he simply disciplines. His arms are always open to you even when the arms of everyone else around you are folded in contemptable pride.

However, please have an honest, accurate, and reflective look in the mirror to ensure the outcome of Edom doesn't also fall on you. For as verse 15 states: "The day of the Lord is near for all nations. As you have done, it will be done to you; your deeds will return upon your own head."

You reap what you sow.

Jonah

Big Idea

God's grace can grasp those too far gone.

Author

Most likely Jonah wrote the book that bears his name.

Original Recipients

The original recipient was the nation of Israel as they were dealing with hatred toward the Assyrian empire that was soon to overtake them.

Date of Writing

If Jonah recorded the book, it was written sometime during the eighth century BCE before Assyria led the northern kingdom of Israel into exile. Some scholars debate this, but the preexilic date is most likely correct.

Historical Setting/Timeline of Events

Jonah witnessed the repentance of Nineveh through his preaching during the reign of Jeroboam II who ruled the northern kingdom of Israel from 793 to 753 BCE. Understanding this historical timeframe is critical if one desires to truly grasp the hard-hitting point of the book. Nineveh wasn't just another city containing God's people like most prophets were addressing at the time. No, no … in contrast, Nineveh was the capital of Assyria—the most fierce, hated, and pagan enemy of Israel. As a matter of fact, it would only be a few decades later that Assyria would turn on God's people and lead them into captivity! This explains why Jonah so badly hated preaching to them!

Main Characters

Jonah and the people of Nineveh serve as the main characters. However, the overall purpose of the book teaches us more about God than it does either of our main characters. More about that below under "Purpose."

Purpose

This book of prophecy is unique in that it contains only a single line of prophecy. The rest is simply narrative. The narrative opens with a man named Jonah being called by God to preach repentance to his enemy Assyria (Nineveh specifically, which was the capital city). Jonah, like his fellow Israelites, hated the Assyrians for their pagan and fierce nature. Furthermore, Israel could feel the tension building on the world scene as Assyria was conquering all in her path. Jonah's perspective was very likely: "Why would I preach to the very people that are preparing to overtake us?"

To take matters into his own hands, Jonah boarded a ship headed the opposite direction. An intense storm arose, and to save the boat and crew, Jonah instructed them to throw him overboard. After a quick bath in the sea, God sent a great fish to swallow Jonah. Three days and nights Jonah spent in the belly of the fish *as he was transported back toward Nineveh by God*. After being vomited back onto the shore, Jonah finally decided to obey and marched to Nineveh.

Upon arrival he spoke to the Ninevites and proclaimed the only line of prophecy contained in the entire book: "Forty more days and Nineveh will be overthrown" (Jonah 3:4). As he suspected, the Assyrians repented, and God spared them. This drove Jonah to madness as he exclaimed to God that he knew He was compassionate, slow to anger, and abounding in love. Jonah was so fed up with their salvation that he asked God to kill him! Jonah went out to the edge of town where God caused a leafy plant to grow up and provide Jonah shade. Jonah was very happy about the plant, but at dawn the next day God sent a worm that killed it. The sun scorched down on Jonah, and once again he wanted to die. Chapter 4 continues with Jonah talking back to God. In 4:9 God asked, "Is it right for you to be angry about the plant?" Jonah responded in the same verse: "It is," he said. "And I'm so angry I wish I were dead." The Lord's response to Jonah's childish response drives home the overarching point of the entire book. In 4:10–11 God replies: "You have been concerned about this plant, though you did not tend it or make it grow. It sprang up overnight and died overnight. And should I not have concern for the great city of Nineveh, in which there are more than a 120,000 people who cannot tell their right hand from their left—and also many animals?"

In other words, Jonah and the nation of Israel were being taught a very important lesson: God's grace, mercy, and forgiveness is for *all* people who repent! Other prophets like Joel, Amos, and Obadiah had condemned other nations like Assyria, which may have inadvertently led

God's people to become very nationalistic and prejudiced. God's people knew they were chosen by Him. Yet, they lacked the understanding that God wasn't just providing salvation to them; in fact, God was simply using them as the vehicle to provide salvation to all people and nations—including Assyria! Therefore, "Jonah proves that indeed God does love and care for even the Assyrians, the most vicious and powerful of all Israel's ancient enemies."[96]

Key Scripture(s) and Theme(s)

Chapter 4 concludes the book and, as a whole, serves as the key scripture depicting the main theme that God's compassion, mercy, and grace extend to all people who repent.

Contemporary Application

Many applications can be derived from the book of Jonah such as the vital importance of not running from God and obedience to His call. However, in keeping with the bigger picture of the book, the main application we take from this book is the simple fact that God cares about every single human being *regardless of what we think about them.*

Let's be real; I am just simply not fond of some people. There are people that you and I do not like. Some of us even have hatred in our hearts for others. But regardless of how badly we dislike someone, God wants to see his or her soul in heaven! And this is what it means when we say that *God's grace can grasp those too far gone.*

Every single human on Earth has been made in the image of God, and He desires fellowship with them. Certainly, some people are rotten creatures and have given in to their cruel and sinful nature. Humans commit unbelievable atrocities daily. But even the most degenerate of murderers, thieves, rapists, kidnappers, drug dealers, child abusers, and human traffickers deserve a shot at the grace and forgiveness of our great and merciful God. Honestly, this doesn't always set well with me as sometimes I've felt like some folks deserve swift and crushing justice. Nonetheless, God loves each of us the same. This is something I cannot fully grasp, and I really want to disagree with at times. But I'm so very

---

[96] Paul R. House, *Old Testament Theology* (Downers Grove, IL: Intervarsity Press, 1998.), 441.

glad God has had mercy on my wretched soul. All we can do is hope *all* others accept God's mercy, regardless of how we personally feel about them.

God's grace can grasp those too far gone.

Micah

Big Idea

It *really* matters that we worship God properly.

And it *really* matters that we treat one another properly.

Author

Micah, a prophet from Moresheth, most likely a town in Judah.

Original Recipients

The original recipients of this book were the leadership and people of the northern kingdom of Israel and the southern kingdom of Judah.

Date of Writing

"Micah's prophetic ministry in writing can be dated between 735 and 700 BCE."[97]

Historical Setting/Timeline of Events

"Micah's prophecies began at least a decade before the fall of Samaria in 722 BCE. He prophesied during the reigns of Jotham (750–731 BCE), Ahaz (743–715 BCE), and Hezekiah (728–686 BCE)."[98] This was a time of great economic prosperity but spiritual bankruptcy for both the northern kingdom of Israel and the southern kingdom of Judah. So, in an effort to lead God's people back to where they belonged, Micah joined with his contemporary prophets of Isaiah and Amos and preached a stern message to his eighth century BCE audience.

Main Characters

The leadership and people of the northern kingdom of Israel and the southern kingdom of Judah serve not only as the original recipients but also the main characters. Their enemy, the great and powerful Assyria, is also a main character.

---

[97] Robert B. Hughes and J. Carl Laney, *Tyndale Concise Bible Commentary* (Wheaton, IL: Tyndale House, 1990.), 351.

[98] Ibid., 351.

Purpose

Under the reigns of King Jeroboam II of Israel (786–746 BCE) and King Uzziah of Judah (783–742 BCE) the two kingdoms became almost as expansive and influential on the world scene as the days of King Solomon.[99] Great riches abounded, and luxury was the norm for many. However, two issues condemned in the book of Micah threatened to end this great time of achievement. First, the wealthy class was becoming richer at the expense of the poor—highly condemned not only in Micah but all throughout the prophets and scripture. Second, paganism had crept into their spirituality. The Canaanite worship and idolatry of the surrounding nations had dug a foothold and considerably influenced the spiritual fabric of God's people. At this point one might assume the idolatry was condemned more harshly, *but the reality is that Micah spent significantly more time addressing the social injustices of his day.* According to Micah, these two issues, with an emphasis more on the social injustice, would lead to Israel's captivity in 721 BCE by the Assyrians followed by Judah's captivity by the Babylonians in 586 BCE.

Key Scripture(s) and Theme(s)

Three options have been given to us by theologians regarding the structure of the book and its thematic contents. The first option divides the book into Micah 1–3, 4–5, and 6–7. Based on this structure, chapters 1–3 focus on the theme of God holding the Israelites and Gentiles accountable for their sins while preserving a remnant for His sake. Chapters 4 and 5 center on the theme of a Davidic ruler being sent in the future to save the remnant. Chapters 6 and 7 conclude the book by presenting the theme of God keeping His covenant made with Abraham and providing salvation to the remnant through His upholding of the Abrahamic covenant.

The second organizational option adopted by theologians is to divide the book into chapters 1–5 and 6–7. The former focuses on the sins of the entire world, and the latter zooms in on the sins of Israel.

The last option is not structured thematically as are the other two. Instead, this structure divides the book into three distinct sections each beginning with a new call to "hear" (1:2, 3:1, 6:1). Following this method,

---

[99] Thomas Edward McComiskey, "Micah," in *The Expositor's Bible Commentary*, vol. 7, ed. Frank E. Gaebelein (Grand Rapids, MI: Zondervan, 1985), 395.

we see a "summons to hear, followed by an oracle of doom, and ending with a statement of hope."[100]

I personally prefer the latter of the three structures. It seems to provide a better context to simply allow Micah to say what he had to say. It approaches Micah from a more "biblical theology" perspective than a "systematic theology" approach. Nothing is wrong with "systematic theology," but the purpose of this book is rooted in more of a "biblical theology" perspective than the latter. (If you have not already done so, I highly recommend each reader familiarize themselves with the differences between "biblical theology" and "systematic theology." Both are just as valid as the other and are critically required for a proper understanding of scripture).

Contemporary Application

At the end of the day, for the contemporary Christian we have two main points of application given to us by Micah: (1) it *really* matters that we worship God properly, and (2) it *really* matters that we treat one another properly.

Micah addresses both realities but, surprising to most, *he spends more time addressing how we treat one another.* In Micah's day this was pointed out specifically at how the rich were exploiting the poor. The rich continued to become wealthier while the poor continued to become poorer. Unfortunately, we all have a front-row seat in observing this same atrocious sin in our modern times—we know too well what that looks like in our society today. In so many ways the poor are utilized as mere tools by the rich to pile up larger and larger heaps of glamorous garbage.

The data-driven, undeniably provable, fact-based list of ways this is accomplished is ridiculously long and reeks of the stench of corruption. Whether it be politicians on both sides of the aisle, corporate America's inclination to lay off large numbers of workers simply to meet an arbitrary quarterly goal or just a small transaction between two individuals, the poor of our society have certainly been dealt an unfair hand in many ways. This is wrong, and God will deal with it in His own time. So, if you've been dealt that unfair hand, please hold onto the strong arm of God and

---

[100] Ibid., 397.

continue to press through with Him. On the contrary, if you're the guilty hand in this matter, *there is no way you get away with this.*

We all know what fake and tainted worship looks like. We all know what wrongful treatment of others looks like. This is what we mean when we say:

It *really* matters that we worship God properly.

And it *really* matters that we treat one another properly.

Nahum

Big Idea

The One True God decides and directs the destinies of *all* nations.

Author

Nahum.

Original Recipients

The original recipients were both the northern kingdom of Israel and the southern kingdom of Judah.

Date of Writing

The context of Nahum clearly depicts Assyria as the main world power at the time. Assyria didn't start to decline in power and lose its grip on the ancient world until after the death of their king Ashurbanipal. Therefore, we can estimate with quite certainty that Nahum was written sometime during his reign between 660–633 BCE. Many scholars believe it was written sometime around 650 BCE.[101]

Historical Setting/Timeline of Events

Assyria was clearly the world power during most of the 600s BCE. They had extended their domination down into Egypt, including the Palestinian region of God's people. Ashurbanipal, the king of Assyria, was in complete control of God's people and had made Manasseh the puppet king of Judah, ruling from 697 to 642 BCE (2 Kings 21:1–18, 2 Chronicles 33:1–20). Manasseh was forced to provide military assistance in Assyria's domination over Egypt. All these events and the entire prophecy of Nahum took place prior to 612 BCE—a date that will be discussed later.[102]

---

[101] Robert B. Hughes and J. Carl Laney, *Tyndale Concise Bible Commentary* (Wheaton, IL: Tyndale House, 1990), 355.
[102] Ibid.

Main Characters

Although God is ultimately the main character in every book of the Bible, Nahum clearly depicts God and His trait of justice as the main character of the book.

Purpose

Unfortunately, Jonah's preaching to Nineveh, the Assyrian capital, and their quick response of repentance was short lived. Just about a century after Jonah's experience, Nahum entered the scene and called out the sins of a wicked and extremely vicious Assyria. At this point, Assyria was clearly the world power and had led military campaigns to conquer more and more territory with the use of excessive and never-before-seen violence. The people of God had fallen to Assyria and had grown very weary of their atrocious circumstances.

In response, God sent Nahum to prophesy to His precious people to remind them that while the Assyrians seemed unbeatable, they were absolutely going to be held responsible for their sins. This eventually took place in 612 BCE "when Nineveh was destroyed by the Babylonian and Median armies."[103]

However, the events of Nahum took place prior to the Assyrian fall, and God's people had no ability to forecast it. Therefore, they were downcast and without hope as they were surrounded by the overwhelming cloud of Assyria's brute force and treacherous violent temper. God reminded them, through Nahum, that He alone was all-powerful and ruled with complete authority over the world scene. The people of God were reminded and encouraged by the fact that God had never lost control. He was still deciding, directing, and dictating the destinies of all nations. They were assured that the Assyrians were going to answer to God for their evil ways. Therefore, the people of God were to remain hopeful for a brighter future.

God consoled His people.

Key Scripture(s) and Theme(s)

Nahum 1:2–3a wraps up the entire message of Nahum with frank and direct simplicity: "The Lord is a jealous and avenging God; the Lord takes vengeance and is filled with wrath. The Lord takes vengeance on his foes

---

[103] Ibid.

and vents His wrath against his enemies. The Lord is slow to anger but great in power; the Lord will not leave the guilty unpunished."

Contemporary Application

Our contemporary world consists of one great performance after another of injustices at the national and international level. We see this in the news on our televisions and smart devices every day. We see it with politicians playing their games at the expense and detriment of the people. We see it as nations pit themselves against one another costing many people their lives and livelihoods. The national and international scene tends to simply repeat itself throughout history. However, we can clearly maintain hope through whatever our century of injustice introduces to us because we know that all things fall under the scrutiny of the almighty God. No matter how big or powerful the overwhelming force may seem, no nation is exempt from the accountability of God.

One aspect that is vital to understand if we are to apply Nahum correctly is to remember that *Nahum specifically deals with the international scene.* He looks at our circumstances more from a global perspective. So, while we may be able to find application from Nahum into injustices done on a smaller scale, we would be wise to remember the international nature of Nahum's address. The bigger picture of God being in full control of our entire planet is the subject of Nahum's address.

God certainly has your specific individual circumstances in His hand, and that is solidified by the fact that He has the entire planet in His hands. As a matter of fact, if the book of Nahum were to be summarized in a children's song, it would have to be the well-known "He's Got the Whole World in His Hands."

At the end of the day, Nahum teaches us that we can rest our head on our pillow and sleep in *comfort* despite the *discomforts* of the day. Nahum gives us permission to do this because it teaches that God records everything. And one day that recording will be called into account, and all injustices will be served justice. No one is powerful enough to escape this, for *the One True God decides and directs the destinies of all nations.*

Go in peace. God's got this.

Habakkuk

Big Idea

God can be trusted.

Author

Not much is known of the author other than that his name was Habakkuk.

Original Recipients

Habakkuk was originally written to the southern kingdom of Judah as she was about to enter Babylonian captivity during the early sixth century BCE.

Date of Writing

Habakkuk 1:5–11 presents the Babylonian captivity as futuristic; it had not yet taken place. The Babylonians came into power in 605 BCE, so this section was likely written sometime just prior to this. However, other sections of Habakkuk (1:12–17 and 2:6–20) indicate that they may have been written sometime after the Babylonians were already a feared foe. In the end it can be determined that it may have been written "over a long period of time, possibly beginning as early as 626 and continuing as late as 590 or after."[104]

Historical Setting/Timeline of Events

"Habakkuk's prophecy is set against a background of the decline and fall of the Judean kingdom (626–586 BCE)."[105] Judah, unlike her brother Israel to the north, had narrowly escaped the great armies of the Assyrians just a century or so prior. But now, God was going to use the dreadful and wretched hand of Babylon as the rod of discipline toward Judah. He was going to use Babylon to call His people back to Him through repentance.

Main Characters

---

[104] Carl E. Armerding, "Habakkuk," in *The Expositor's Bible Commentary*, vol. 7, ed. Frank E. Gaebelein (Grand Rapids, MI: Zondervan, 1985), 493.
[105] Ibid.

God, Habakkuk, Judah, and Babylon all serve as main characters.

Purpose

Habakkuk began his ministry as a prophet in the late seventh century BCE. By that time, Judah was already too familiar with the marching cadence of the horrific Babylonian army, and God was apparently giving His nod of approval. Or was He?

Though the people of God had spent the last several centuries proving their disloyalty to God, they did not seem to draw the connection between their unfaithfulness and their undoing. They were asking the question: "Why is God allowing this to happen to His people?!" And this very question is what Habakkuk asked God. Thankfully, we have recorded in the book of Habakkuk God's unrivaled and unchallenged reply.

In addition to discipline, great hope is found in Habakkuk. God communicated that even though Babylon was being used to punish Judah, she too would pay for her sins! In other words, God was going to prove Himself to be trustworthy because He was fair in His judgments. God was communicating through Habakkuk that those who serve Him would prosper, but those who deny Him would experience His wrath.

The book, then, unfolds in four sections to convey this message. Paul R. House, in his book *Old Testament Theology*, unpacks this quite nicely:

> First, 1:2–11 demonstrates that God will punish Israel by sending Babylon to chastise them. This God reveals the future. Second, 1:12–2:11 states that Yahweh expects faith from the faithful as Babylon is punished for their sins. Third, 2:12–20 makes it clear that Yahweh crushes idolaters. Neither Israel nor Babylon can stand against the one God by serving images. Fourth, 3:1–19 claims that Yahweh always acts on behalf of the faithful. The prophet may take refuge in God's power.[106]

---

[106] Paul R. House, *Old Testament Theology* (Downers Grove, IL: Intervarsity Press, 1998), 376.

Key Scripture(s) and Theme(s)

The critical point of Habakkuk is found in 2:4. "See, the enemy is puffed up; his desires are not upright—but the righteous person will live by his faithfulness."

This verse so profoundly shapes the concept of wholeheartedly placing one's faith in God that it was quoted three times in the New Testament. In Romans 1:17 Paul stated that salvation is through faith in Jesus and cited Habakkuk 2:4 as his authority. Paul then, in Galatians 3:11–12, contrasted the law with faith in Jesus and again fell back on Habakkuk 2:4 as his biblical proof. Lastly, 2:4 is quoted by the writer of Hebrews in 10:37–38 tying it to faith in Jesus Christ to comfort the heavily persecuted church.[107]

Contemporary Application

Have you ever looked up into the skies and wondered, in utter confusion, "What are you up to, Lord? I don't understand what you're doing, God." If so, you're not alone. Have you ever wondered why you, as a believer, were suffering at the hands of the ungodly? If so, you're still not alone.

Sometimes we don't understand the hand of God simply because we do not see the big picture—we cannot always see God's purpose in the whole of human history. Furthermore, it can become especially difficult when we become confined to the tunnel vision our dire circumstances demand. Sometimes our difficulties are a result of our own sin. Other times, our bumps and bruises are no fault of our own. Regardless, we can see in Habakkuk that God is fair in all His ways. We can trust in God and know that He makes all things right in the end. Even when we're being disciplined by God due to our own sin, His ways are always pure, fair, and just.

God's task is to manage and maintain the cosmos. Our task is to trust Him. We certainly do not have the ability to grasp the complexity with which He easily works ... so all we can do is trust the One who has no rival. "While history is still awaiting its conclusion ... the righteous ones

---

[107] Carl E. Armerding, "Habakkuk," in *The Expositor's Bible Commentary,* vol. 7, ed. Frank E. Gaebelein (Grand Rapids, MI: Zondervan, 1985), 495.

are to live by faith."[108] And the required twenty-six hundred years ago during the time of Habakkuk is the same faith required today.

This is not always easy, but it is God's way. Stick with Him no matter the circumstances, and He will see you through it all! God can be trusted.

---

[108] Ibid., 496–97.

Zephaniah

Big Idea

The rebellious are ruined, but the repentant are restored!

Author

Zephaniah, like many Old Testament prophets, opens by naming its author. But in contrast to most prophets, this book tracks his lineage all the way back to his great-great grandfather King Hezekiah. Zephaniah 1:1 states that the prophet was "the son of Cushi, the son of Gedaliah, the son of Amariah, the son of Hezekiah." This was very intentional as it was King Hezekiah that served God faithfully amid a line of kings that had forsaken Him. In essence, just as King Hezekiah was juxtaposed to his unfaithful comrades as he led Judah back to God, Zephaniah was called to do the same.

Original Recipients

Zephaniah 1:1 states that Zephaniah originally prophesied to Judah during the reign of King Josiah (640–609 BCE), who listened to the prophet's words and led his people into a time of short-lived faithfulness.

Date of Writing

Josiah's reign is outlined in 2 Chronicles 34–35. He reigned thirty-one years (2 Chronicles 34:1) from 640 to 609 BCE.[109] It can be determined that Zephaniah wrote the book titled after his name sometime around that period in the late seventh century BCE.

Historical Setting/Timeline of Events

The godly years of David's reign took place two decades on both sides of 1,000 BCE. They were characterized by blessing, prosperity, and economic growth. However, by the time Zephaniah's ministry was needed, the days of David's reign and subsequent blessings were long gone. After David's son King Solomon died in 931 BCE, the nation of Israel was

---

[109] David S. Dockery, gen ed., *Holman Concise Bible Commentary* (Nashville, TN: B&H Publishing, 1998, 2010), 377.

split into two smaller nations—the northern kingdom of Israel and the southern kingdom of Judah.

Both nations quickly fell into deep sin and rebellion to God, which resulted in the northern kingdom going away forever into Assyrian captivity in 721 BCE. However, God's plan for salvation was not to be thwarted. The Davidic lineage continued its trail through history cloaked within the southern kingdom of Judah. It was through this lineage that ultimate salvation would one day come through Jesus Christ.

Yet even though Judah would one day produce the Messiah, they were certainly not absent from rebellion and idolatry. Though some of her kings were godly, most failed to lead the people as God desired. One of the worst of these kings, Manasseh, had rebuilt the pagan altars his father, Hezekiah, had destroyed. He even sacrificed his own children on these altars. After his death, his son Amon became king and continued in the sins of his father. However, due to a coup and a successful assassination attempt, Amon's reign lasted only two years. His son Josiah became king at the age of eight years. It was this young King Josiah to whom the prophet Zephaniah prophesied. Thankfully, Josiah listened. He served God and brought about great reforms for the kingdom of God. Nonetheless, this was short lived, causing the warnings of Zephaniah to eventually become a reality.

For a parallel reading in the historical books, please see 2 Kings 21–23:30 and 2 Chronicles 33–35.

Main Characters

The main characters of Zephaniah are Zephaniah, King Josiah, and the southern kingdom of Judah. Also, the entire world is a supporting character as represented by the lands of Philistia, Moab, and Ammon, Cush, and Assyria.

Purpose

As stated in the "Historical Setting/Timeline of Events," we find a rebellious people being addressed by Zephaniah. He was calling out their most extreme unfaithfulness. God was very clear on three points in this book as He addressed the late seventh century unfaithfulness.

1. Rebellion will be annihilated with absolute resolve (Zephaniah 1:2–18).
2. Judah should repent because *all* nations will be judged (Zephaniah 2:1–3:8).
3. The repentant remnant will be rescued and restored (Zephaniah 3:9–20).

In 721 BCE Judah watched as their brothers in the northern kingdom of Israel were marched into Assyrian captivity *due to their sins*. Yet, Judah failed to implement a plan to prevent the same outcome in their lives. So, Zephaniah stepped up as prophet and led them back to repentance, though it be only for a brief time. He did this by speaking to young King Josiah, which led to a rediscovery of the law and incredible religious reforms.

Key Scripture(s) and Theme(s)

Three key themes found within Zephaniah have been previously stated above under the purpose.

Contemporary Application

Is truth relative? Zephaniah exclaims no! Yet, contemporary society has fully embraced a relativistic worldview that asserts that each individual determines his or her own truth. In other words, truth is not an outward force that we are to discover but rather something that is generated from within each person. Have you ever heard someone say, "Well, that may be true for you, but it's not true for me." Or maybe, "Well, if that's your conviction you should follow it, but it's just not what I believe, so I don't have to."

Godless statements like this are uttered daily, even by Christians. However, universal acceptance of an idea does *not* make it true. At the end of the day, all nations and people groups will be judged by God—by the One who determines truth. Whoever is found to be out of touch with the reality of God's truth will be ruined, but those who have aligned themselves with God's truth will be restored. The rebellious are ruined, but the repentant are restored! This is how we apply Zephaniah's words into our contemporary lives and society.

Zephaniah teaches us that rebellion to God will be judged with a finality that will leave the entire Earth *speechless*. No one will be able to raise a fist or a voice to the authority contained in God's dictation of reality! Those who have previously shouted "it's all relative!" will be so heavily quieted by the absolute hand of God. This will not be a good day for many of us, and I pray for mercy on our souls.

However, we can also be greatly encouraged through Zephaniah's words! His message reaches through over twenty-six hundred years of history and makes two additional encouraging points very clear to us twenty-first century believers:

1. If we've abandoned God and His nonnegotiable ways, we can repent! (Zephaniah 2:1–7).
2. While ruin certainly comes to the rebellious, restoration comes to the repentant! (Zephaniah 3:9–20).

In the end, Zephaniah was serving alongside many other biblical characters. He was called to play his part—in his generation—to move humanity closer and closer to the time of the Messiah. Just like he served God faithfully, we are to also serve Him … to play our part … in our generation … to move humanity closer and closer to their time when God brings about His ultimate plan of salvation through Jesus Christ.

Haggai[110]

Big Idea
Failure is not an option.

Author
Haggai the prophet (Haggai 1:1).

Original Recipients
The original recipients of Haggai's prophecies were God's people of Judah after they had been taken into Babylonian captivity. They had been given permission from Persia's new ruler, Darius (521–486 BCE), to rebuild Jerusalem and the temple. Specifically, Haggai spoke most directly to Zerubbabel, the governor; Joshua, the priest; and the religious leaders.

Date of Writing
Haggai began prophesying "in the second year of King Darius" (1:1). Darius ruled Persia from 521 to 486 BCE, so Haggai began his work in 520 BCE.[111]

Historical Setting/Timeline of Events
The glory days of the great pagan nation Assyria had long come and gone—and their captives, the northern kingdom of Israel, no longer existed. Babylon had also experienced its rise and fall and, in 539 BCE, succumbed to the new world power of Persia. This was good news for Judah as their ruthless captor Babylon was no longer in charge. With Persia conquering Babylon, they, by default, assumed all those in submission to Babylon including God's people Judah.

While Babylon had assimilated Judah into their culture forcing their ways upon them, this new era of Persian rule introduced religious tolerance. Judah was given the opportunity to return to true worship. Cyrus, the king

---

[110] Haggai and Zechariah were contemporaries of one another whose messages worked in close tandem with one another. It is best to study them together to see the bigger picture of what God was doing at the end of the 500s BC among His people.
[111] Joyce G. Baldwin, *Haggai, Zechariah, Malachi: An Introduction and Commentary, Tyndale Old Testament Commentary Series* (Downers Grove IL: InterVarsity, 1972), 29.

of Persia, allowed the exiled Jews to return to their homeland and rebuild Jerusalem and its temple. However, opposition arose from their neighbors that held influence in the Persian court, and the work was stopped about 534–535 BCE. (Ezra 4:4–6:22). About fifteen or sixteen years later, King Darius assumed the Persian throne. It was at this point, in 520 BCE, that the prophet Haggai (as well as Zechariah) began to urge the Jews to finish what they had started.

Main Characters

Haggai, the prophet; Zerubabbel, the governor; Joshua, the high priest; and the people of Judah are the main characters of Haggai.

Purpose

Haggai prophesied to Judah to inspire them to finish rebuilding the temple in Jerusalem. He "intertwines restoration and the temple reconstruction. He identifies the rebuilding project as the *key initial step that will transform the past of curse to the future of blessing* flowing from God's renewed presence."[112] You see, they had previously been in Babylonian captivity and were not allowed to worship God as He intended. However, when Persia conquered Babylon in 539 BCE, Judah became subject to Persia.

It was the relaxed policy of Persia to allow their captors to practice their own culture and spirituality if they properly paid homage. They were basically free to live according to their customs if they honored Persia as their authority.

Key Scripture(s) and Theme(s)

Haggai communicated his message to finish the previous work on the temple in four sermons, each with its own theme.

First, he *proclaimed a call for adjusted priorities* in 1:1–15. Verse 4 states: "Is it a time for you yourselves to be living in your paneled houses, while this house remains a ruin?" In other words, they had built their own homes to meet their satisfaction but had abandoned God's house. He told them that this was the reason for their less-than-desirable crop yields, poor food,

---

[112] Mark J. Boda, "Haggai, Zechariah," In *NIV Application Commentary*, ed. Terry C. Muck (Grand Rapids, MI: Zondervan, 2004), 11.

ragged clothes, and weakening economy. This spurred them into action as work on the temple began.

Second, about a month after his call for adjusted priorities, Haggai *encouraged them by stating that God was with them* (2:1–9). There was definite discouragement among the rebuilding because their temple wasn't near as glorious as was the temple of King Solomon's day. Haggai saw this would be a detriment, so he addressed this very directly by asking them to compare the two temples. This gave them an opportunity to voice their discouragement. Upon hearing their dire response, Haggai encouraged them to continue despite its lackluster appearance because *God was still with them*. His blessing was upon the project.

Haggai addressed the priests in a third sermon about two months after his second sermon. Here he communicated *that God's blessing was now upon them despite their past unfaithfulness* (2:10–19). Here Haggai asked them if sacred meat would remain holy if it indirectly touched other food. Their response was no. Haggai then asked them another simple question in 2:13: "If a person defiled by contact with a dead body touches one of these things, does it become defiled?" They answered yes. With this response Haggai explained to them that this means righteousness doesn't rub off onto unrighteousness—rather unrighteousness more easily taints the holy things. This was a powerful illustration to them as they needed to understand that sin was more contagious than righteousness. The lesson was that it was easier to fall into sin than it was to live a holy life before God. Haggai explained to the priests (and to the people indirectly) that they and all they offered God was defiled.

But this was only half of the message contained within sermon three. Haggai explains in 2:15–19 that God had withheld blessings because of their defilement, but he would no longer do this: "From this day on I will bless you" (2:19). Hope and blessings were beginning to flow *from their obedience* in rebuilding the temple.

In the last sermon, outlined in 2:20–23, Haggai directly addressed Zerubbabel with *hope and encouragement of the coming Messiah*. He stated: "'On that day,' declares the Lord Almighty, 'I will take you, my servant Zerubbabel son of Shealtiel,' declares the Lord, 'and I will make you like my signet right, for I have chosen you,' declares the Lord Almighty'" (2:23). God encouraged Zerubbabel by reminding him that he was of the lineage of David, through whom the Messiah would come and bring ultimate peace to not only Judah but also to the world.

Contemporary Application

Two main applications will be outlined here from Haggai.

First, God promised to save His people from themselves. He did this, ultimately, through His Son Jesus Christ. However, He used the entirety of the Old Testament to set the stage for Christ's coming. Each phase of the Old Testament brought its assigned puzzle piece of God's plan leading to the time when it was right for Jesus to appear (Galatians 4:4). Haggai and the folks of his day were no different. Haggai showed that the lineage of Zerubbabel and the work accomplished rebuilding the temple through his leadership were being used to bring about the Messiah. In other words, God had a plan to save us, and it was not going to fail! This was true in Haggai's day, and it is also true in our day. God is going to finish what He started in us!

God simply cannot and will not fail, period. Yes, the folks in Haggai's day were filled with discouragement and hopelessness—the very same feelings we sometimes have today. But God didn't fail then, and He absolutely and unequivocally will not fail today. He has no rival, period, even when it seems like life isn't turning out the way you thought it would (this is exactly what the people thought in Haggai).

God has always been in control, and He has never allowed His plan to fail. We can trace this throughout the Bible: Joseph was sold into slavery by his brothers and eventually was thrown into Egyptian prison. The Israelites were in Egyptian slavery for four hundred years. Moses, a prince of Egypt, lived in desert exile for forty years. David, the king of Israel, ran for his life as his son was trying to kill him. The Assyrians conquered the northern kingdom of Israel. Babylon conquered the southern kingdom of Judah. These and so many more biblical happenings serve as examples of what appeared to be God's abandonment of His people. But He was always there dictating the world scene to ultimately lead the world to Jesus Christ.

He is doing the same thing with us today.

Regardless of our situations, God is setting up inside us His plan. He is still steering the hearts of world leaders, good and evil, to bring about His kingdom. And friends, God doesn't know the sting of failure.

Also, going back to the Big Idea, when God gives us a task to accomplish, He expects us to finish it. Failure is not an option. Those in the Old Testament were looking forward to the coming of the Messiah while we look back at the Messiah. Yet our work for God is the same. Ultimately, everything in the Old Testament was accomplished to introduce people to Jesus Christ. Likewise, everything in the New Testament was accomplished to introduce people to Jesus Christ. And last, everything in our day is to be accomplished to introduce people to Jesus Christ. It doesn't matter what side of the timeline we're on—we all have our small part to play in God's overarching plan to bring people to salvation through Jesus. Again, failure is not an option.

So often we look at the characters of the Bible and assign to them some sort of special power or spiritual glow that we simply don't have. This is incorrect thinking and needs assured adjustment. Old Testament people were scratching and clawing for every inch gained in life just like us. They experienced the same failures, difficulties, and doubts we have. However, one thing we all have in common regardless of what century we're working in is that we all have the same authority of the Creator of the cosmos. When we fall in line with God's plan, we are plunged into the unstoppable river of *His* authority.

Continue through the struggles, joys, failures, successes, difficulties, shortcomings, and all the ups and downs of serving God, and you will come through victorious!

Stay strong and carry on—finish what He has called you to start.

God finishes what He starts, and He has equipped and called us to do the same.

Push forward!

Failure is not an option for God, and failure is not an option for us.

Zechariah[113]

Big Idea

Complying to God's command creates comfort in the chaos.

Author

Zechariah wrote the book named after him. "Like Jeremiah and Ezekiel, Zechariah was a priest as well as a prophet."[114]

Original Recipients

The original recipients were the discouraged people of God as they were under Persian control in the late sixth century BCE.

Date of Writing

Most theologians agree that Zechariah, as well as Haggai, were written shortly after the dates given by each prophet in their introductions. Zechariah 1:1 states that the Lord first spoke to him "in the eighth month of the second year of Darius (520 BCE) as well as another time two years later, as 7:1 states: "in the fourth year of Darius" (518 BCE).[115]

Historical Setting/Timeline of Events

There were truly no real glory days for God's people throughout the Old Testament after the destruction of the temple in 586 BCE. Yet God was still working and steering His people throughout this tumultuous time of despair and discouragement. Though David's great reign and Solomon's elaborate temple were long gone, God was still fully in charge and directing the affairs of the world. Zechariah was one of the key figures God used to continue His plan of salvation throughout this postexilic world.

So much was taking place on the world scene during this time. World powers were shifting. Instability and unpredictability were perfect

---

[113] Zechariah worked alongside Haggai, so it would be worth going back and reading the previous pages of Haggai if you have not already done so. Although their messages have differences, they were addressing the same issue from different angles.

[114] David S. Dockery, gen. ed., *Holman Concise Bible Commentary* (Nashville: B&H Publishing, 2010), 384.

[115] Mark J. Boda, "From Fasts to Feasts: The Literary Function of Zechariah 7–8," *CBQ* 65 (2003): 403–4.

descriptors for the future for Judah. Yet, as always, God was in charge of even the greatest of world leaders. He moved upon them to allow His people to return to Jerusalem to rebuild their temple and hopefully rebuild their hearts.

During Zechariah's day (late sixth century BCE), God's people answered to and paid homage to the great Persians. This was much more tolerable as the Persians were more liberal on their foreign policy than Judah's initial captors—the fearsome Babylonians. It was due to this tolerance that they were allowed to return to Jerusalem to rebuild and worship the One True God under the direction of Ezra, Nehemiah, and Zerubbabel.

Main Characters

Zechariah, the people of Judah, and a loving God are the main characters.

Purpose

Although Haggai and Zechariah were contemporaries of one another, their messages were different. "Whereas Haggai's focus was on the rebuilding of the temple and the reinstitution of the sacrificial system, Zechariah's was on the people's spiritual transformation."[116] While Haggai encouraged Judah to fulfill God's will with the external expression of rebuilding the temple, Zechariah encouraged them to undergo internal transformation to legitimize their outward expression.

These folks had been through a lot. They had been told all the stories of their former glory days under kings David and Solomon. They were taught how beautiful the temple had been when it was at the apex of its grandeur. Yet, over four hundred years of disobedience, desecration, devastation, destruction, and deportation stood between those glory days and the people of Zechariah's time. So, God called Zechariah to prophesy to them to encourage them to return to the Lord with changed hearts.

---

[116] David S. Dockery, gen. ed., *Holman Concise Bible Commentary* (Nashville: B&H Publishing, 2010), 384.

Key Scripture(s) and Theme(s)

"They will be my people, and I will be faithful and righteous to them as their God" (Zechariah 8:8).

"I will say, 'They are my people,' and they will say, 'The Lord is our God'" (Zechariah 13:9).

Contemporary Application

In the books of Haggai and Zechariah we see the broken remnant of God's people as they were trying to make sense of life after spending several generations in the mucky discouragement of exile. *They knew* they were God's people, but it sure didn't seem like *He knew*. So, the two fellows of Haggai and Zechariah brought encouragement to the troubled souls of Judah. Simultaneously they explained that obedience was the only way back to peace with God. "As the remnant community longing for full restoration, the church today is comforted by the proclamation of the character and action of God in these prophets, while at the same time it is challenged by their exhortation to respond to this God through faith and obedience."[117] And so let us learn from Haggai and Zechariah the lesson of obedience and the glorious return to freedom and service to our loving God that follows.

Taking a step back and viewing the prophets allows us to better apply Zechariah's call to obedience. Prior to the Assyrian and Babylonian exiles, God sent His prophets to warn of the impending correction that would fall on them if they didn't make the corrections themselves. They chose to ignore God's warnings, so He sent them into exile to draw them to full repentance and obedience. While the northern kingdom of Israel never recovered, we see God lighten up on the southern kingdom of Judah after seventy years by using Persia to conquer Babylon. Persian rule upon Judah brought about a relaxed form of exile. God was essentially loosening the reins a bit on Judah to see if they had learned obedience. This was the message and heart behind Haggai and Zechariah.

So, when we find ourselves undergoing God's discipline, we can know that a redemptive purpose is always in mind. What His discipline means to us is that we are being redirected by His love with the use of discomfort.

---

[117] Mark J. Boda, "Haggai, Zechariah," In *NIV Application Commentary*, ed. Terry C. Muck (Grand Rapids, MI: Zondervan, 2004), 53.

Unfortunately, for us humans, until the pain to stay the same is greater than the pain to change, we will remain the same. We are stubborn, therefore God's redirection (i.e. His discipline) must sometimes be quite heavy. But when you are in those times, please realize it. When things are rough, and you know it's because you're out of line, please make internal adjustments. This will allow you and I to come out the other side and receive the positive affirmations found in Haggai and Zechariah.

Zechariah teaches us that a great big good God is always on the other side of discipline. He is waiting and wanting us to fall back into His loving embrace. By far, the greatest way I have personally learned this lesson is when I must bring about discipline into my precious five-year-old son's life. It absolutely breaks my heart when Jude must be corrected, but we *always* hug afterward. I always extend my arms out to him and say, "Hug me, hug me!" Through tears he always grips my neck and squeezes hard … only to feel my arms wrap around him in deep embrace.

My son knows my embrace. He knows the strength with which I wrap my protective, hard as nails, loving, kind arms around him, and I can only hope and pray that those strong arms wrapped around him communicate that there is absolutely nothing for Him to fear when he is with his daddy. I pray to God, with tears in my eyes even as I write this, that our embrace following discipline ingrains into his spiritual psychology that God is unimaginably loving, kind, tender, and full of grace even amid discipline.

And that is what it means to say *complying to God's command creates comfort in the chaos.*

Malachi

Big Idea
Internal change must accompany external work.

Author
Malachi the prophet.

Original Recipients
Postexilic Judah was the original recipient of this writing.

Date of Writing
Although Malachi, like many other prophets, does not date his writing, it has been determined by scholars that it was written as a postexilic message to God's people.

Historical Setting/Timeline of Events
Malachi is placed at the end of the Old Testament because that's exactly where it falls chronologically. Most scholars agree that we can place the events of Malachi around 450 BCE, just before or during Ezra's work.[118] What this means is we're dealing with God's people about a century after their return from Babylonian captivity. They were still under the control of Persia, as Persia had conquered Babylon thus assuming all their captors as well. However, Persia allowed them to return to their homeland and rebuild.

Main Characters
God, Postexilic Judah, and Malachi are the main characters.

Purpose
Even at the hands of the Babylonians during their captivity of the seventh and sixth centuries BCE, postexilic Judah had not learned to follow God in obedience. In Malachi's day Ezra, Nehemiah, Zerubbabel, and Haggai had long since performed their work of rebuilding the

---

[118] Robert B. Chisholm, *Interpreting the Minor Prophets* (Grand Rapids, MI: Zondervan, 1990), 278.

temple. Yet, while Haggai's inspiration to rebuild the physical temple had succeeded, Zechariah's intersecting message calling for an internal heart change had not been implemented. Thus, Malachi's purpose was to urge and encourage the people to prepare themselves internally for the coming of God's kingdom.

Upon returning from exile, their hopes were high. They were planning to return to their old way of life by rebuilding the temple and ushering in the next step of God's redemptive plan—the Messiah. However, while the temple had been rebuilt, the kingdom of God was not quite showing up as they had expected. So, the people of God had grown cynical toward Him as they sat in despair. They found themselves asking why God had not fulfilled His side of the covenant when they had fulfilled theirs by rebuilding the temple.

In their minds, the rebuilding of the temple was supposed to be their sign to God for their readiness to experience the ushering in of the Messiah. But it didn't happen as they thought it would. So Malachi stepped up and provided God's reasoning for their continued despondency. Yes, the temple had been rebuilt, but their external return to worship was not accompanied by internal change. The Israelites that returned to rebuild proved to be just as rebellious as their ancestors that were led into the same exile from which they were leaving. At the end of the day, the exile had no real effect on their unfaithfulness.

Key Scripture(s) and Theme(s)

Malachi fulfilled his purpose as outlined above in a way like no other previous prophet. The book is formatted in a series of six disputes that typically begin with God making an accusation regarding their unfaithfulness. This results in Judah's disagreement followed by God offering the last word.

The first three disputes are found in chapters 1 and 2. Here we see God giving the reason for their desperate situation: Israel is still corrupt. The last three disputes are found in chapter 3 and deal specifically with God confronting the corruption he had exposed in the first three disputes. "And the overall impression you get from these arguments and disputes is that the exile fundamentally didn't change anything in the people. Israel's hearts are as hard as ever."[119]

Dispute 1 (1:2–5)

- God communicated that He loved His exiled people.
- They responded by asking "How have you loved us?"
- God demonstrated His love by reminding them He made His covenant through Jacob's lineage instead of Esau's.

Dispute 2 (1:6–2:9)

- God accused them of despising Him by defiling His temple.
- They asked how they had despised Him.
- God pointed out that they had been bringing less than perfect animals for sacrifice.

Dispute 3 (2:10–16)

- God claimed they had been unfaithful to Him as to their wives.
- Israel responded asking how they had done this.
- God stated it was through their idolatry toward Him and through divorce with their wives (also discussed in Nehemiah 13).

Dispute 4 (2:17–3:5)

- Israel asked: "Where is the God of justice? Why have we been abandoned?"
- God responded by saying He would be bringing His Messenger to institute true justice (Messianic reference).

Dispute 5 (3:6–12)

- God beckons them to return to Him.

---

[119] Tim Mackie, "Book of Malachi Summary: A Complete Animated Overview," The Bible Project, August 4, 2016, YouTube video, 1:16, https://youtube.com/watch?v=HPGShWZ4Jvk.

- Israel asks: "How?!"
- God responds by demanding they start paying their tithe and stop stealing from Him.

Dispute 6 (3:13–18)

- Israel exclaimed it was pointless to serve Him because He did nothing about the wicked succeeding.
- God responded by telling a story about how the faithful enjoy talking about how to honor Him. So he orders a scroll to be written so they could read it and reflect on God's character.

After this, God speaks of the future of the faithful.

The last three verses of the book bring a solid conclusion as the people are called to remember the law and prophets as a message of hope calling His people out of rebellion. They were to lose their cynicism toward God and interpret Moses and the prophets as a road map to success.

Contemporary Application

Our external work for God is completely nullified without internal change. We cannot attempt to gain favor from God through our accomplishments—rather our accomplishments must be a result of our internal change.

The last three verses of Malachi teach us that if we are going to experience the necessary internal transformation required to truly know God, we must focus on scripture and its core message. This message exposes us to our own incredibly fallen situation but also explains how God provides a way out!

When we think God is abandoning us, we are to course-correct this false ideology. Instead, we should view God as making a covenant with us (dispute 1) even when we bring him our leftovers (dispute 2). Furthermore, when we are unfaithful to Him and our wives or those around us (dispute 3), God does not abandon us (dispute 4). He is still calling us to Him even when we steal from Him (dispute 5), and He is worthy to be trusted when it feels like the wicked around us are succeeding (dispute 6).

Ultimately, God can be trusted regardless of our circumstances because one day, Malachi exclaims, God will bring about the ultimate restoration of His people by bringing about the Messenger—and we know this Messenger as Jesus Christ.

May your obedience be rooted in faith. Be obedient. Be faithful. Be blessed. Isn't this the point of the Old Testament anyway?

Conclusion

I pray very dearly that this book serves as a springboard for your continued study. In no way is this book intended to be comprehensive. Many times throughout this writing I desired to delve deeper into several concepts but refrained due to the brief nature of this writing. Additionally, I have had to simply decide to submit it for publication as each time I read through it I find areas upon which to edit.

Hopefully, this book will serve to inspire you to dig deeper into God's Word your entire life. One thing I've learned over the years is that no matter how much we learn, there's always someone who is significantly more knowledgeable. I find it very relaxing that God isn't judging me based upon someone else's level of understanding.

We can have all the knowledge in the world, but without humility, God simply won't do much with that knowledge, in us or through us. So, as our biblical knowledge expands, it should naturally drive us to our knees in deeper and deeper humility. In contrast to the false sense of superiority that some individuals seek and feel as they gain knowledge, humbleness is the default position of one who draws closer to our Lord. What other mindset could ever be appropriate when our filth and wretchedness is summoned by God to approach His perfect untouchable holiness? Therefore, we should ask God to pierce not only our minds with the knowledge of His Word but our hearts as well. For without the Person and Work of the Holy Spirit and His illumination of the scriptures in our lives, knowledge is of no use.

In the end, God has revealed enough of Himself in the Bible that we can safely conclude about all things unknown: "I'll just trust Him." The fundamentals are covered. And so, when you find yourself looking up at the stars in a conundrum, go back to the first two lines of this book and say:

Some things are just not for me to know …

… and that's OK.

It's OK because of the Bible.

Works Cited

Allen, Ronald B. "Numbers." In *The Expositor's Bible Commentary,* vol. 2, edited by. Frank E. Gaebelein. Grand Rapids, MI: Zondervan, 1979.

American Bible Society. https://bibleresources.americanbible.org/resource/historical-books, 2023 Philadelphia. Accessed May 4, 2023.

Armerding, Carl E. "Habakkuk." In *The Expositor's Bible Commentary, vol. 7,* edited by Frank E. Gaebelein. Grand Rapids, MI: Zondervan, 1985.

Arnold, Bill T. "1 & 2 Samuel." In *NIV Application Commentary.* Terry C. Muck, ed. Grand Rapids, MI: Zondervan, 2003.

Arnold, Bill T., and Bryan E. Beyer. *Encountering Biblical Studies, Encountering the Old Testament,* edited by Eugene H. Merrill. Grand Rapids, MI: Baker Book House, 1999.

Baldwin, Joyce G. *Haggai, Zechariah, Malachi: An Introduction and Commentary,* Tyndale Old Testament Commentary. Downers Grove, IL: InterVarsity, 1972.

Boda, Mark J. "Haggai, Zechariah." In *NIV Application Commentary,* edited by Terry C. Muck. Grand Rapids, MI: Zondervan, 2004.

Boda, Mark J. "From Fasts to Feasts: The Literary Function of Zechariah 7–8." *CBQ* 65 (2003).

Brand, John D., *A Concise Chronology of the Bible*, Edinburg Bible College, 2004.

Brettler, Mark Zvi. *How to Read The Bible*. Philadelphia: Jewish Publication Society, 2005.

Bright, John. *Jeremiah*, Anchor Bible. Garden City, N.Y.: Doubleday, 1965).

Bubenik, V. "The Rise of Koine." In *A History of Ancient Greek: From the Beginnings to Late Antiquity*, edited by A. F. Christidis. Cambridge: University Press, 2007.

Bullock, C. Hassell. *An Introduction to the Old Testament Poetic Books*. Chicago: Moody, 1979, 1988).

Chisholm, Robert B. *Interpreting the Minor Prophets*. Grand Rapids, MI: Zondervan, 1990.

Constable, Thomas L. "1 Kings." In *The Bible Knowledge Commentary: Old Testament*, edited by John F Walvoord and Roy B. Zuck. Wheaton, IL: Victor Books, 1985.

Dockery, David S., Gen Ed. *Holman Concise Bible Commentary*. Nashville: B&H Publishing, 1998, 2010.

Duguid, Iain M. "Ezekiel." In *The NIV Application Commentary*, edited by Terry Muck. Grand Rapids, MI: Zondervan, 1999.

Fairchild, Mary. "Historical Books." Learn Religions, Aug. 25, 2020, learnreligions.com/historical-books-of-the-bible-700269.

Fredericks, Daniel C. *Qoheleth's Language: Re-evaluating Its Nature and Date* Lewiston, N.Y.: Mellen, 1988.

Holy Bible: NIV Life Application Study Bible, 3rd edition. Grand Rapids, MI: Zondervan, 2020.

Holy Bible: Zondervan Study Bible. Grand Rapids, MI: Zondervan, 2015.

House, Paul R. *Old Testament Theology.* Downers Grove, IL: Intervarsity Press, 1998.

Howard Jr., David M. *An Introduction to the Old Testament Historical Books.* Chicago: Moody, 1993.

Huey Jr., F.B. "Ruth." In *The Expositor's Bible Commentary,* vol. 3, edited by Frank E. Gaebelein. Grand Rapids, MI: Zondervan, 1992.

Hughes, Robert B., and J. Carl Laney. *Tyndale Concise Bible Commentary.* Wheaton, IL: Tyndale House, 1990).

Jobes, Karen H. "When God Spoke Greek: The Place of the Greek Bible in Evangelical Scholarship," BBR 16, 2006.

Keil, C. F. and F. Delitzsch. *Biblical Commentary on the Old Testament - volume 2: Joshua, Judges, Ruth, 1 and 2 Samuel.* Edinburgh: T. & T. Clark, 1857.

Keil, C. F. and F. Delitzsch. *Commentary on the Old Testament,* volume 9: *Ezekiel, Daniel.* By C. F. Keil. Translated by James Martin and M. G. Easton. Peabody: Hendrickson, 1996.

Knoppers, Gary N. and Jonathan S. Greer. *Deuteronomistic History*, edited by C. Matthews. Oxford Bibliography Online: Biblical Studies. New York: Oxford University Press, 2010.

Kreeft, Peter and Ronald Tacelli. *Pocket Handbook of Christian Apologetics.* Westmont: Intervarsity Press, 2003.

Maas, Anthony. *Pentateuch.* In *The Catholic Encyclopedia*, vol. 11. New York: Robert Appleton,1911). 24 Apr. 2021 <http://www.newadvent.org/cathen/11646c.htm>.

Mackie, Tim. "Book of Malachi Summary: A Complete Animated Overview." The Bible Project, August 4, 2016. YouTube video, 1:16. https://youtube.com/watch?v=HPGShWZ4Jvk.

Madvig, Donald H. "Joshua." In *The Expositor's Bible Commentary,* vol. 3, edited by Frank E. Gaebelein. Grand Rapids, MI: Zondervan, 1992.

McComiskey, Thomas Edward. "Micah." In *The Expositor's Bible Commentary,* vol. 7, edited by Frank E. Gaebelein. Grand Rapids, MI: Zondervan, 1985.

Merriam-Webster.com Dictionary, Merriam-Webster, https://www.merriam-webster.com/dictionary/genre. Accessed 1 Jun. 2021.

Merrill, Eugene H. *Kingdom of Priests.* Grand Rapids, MI: Baker Books, 1996.

Neusner, Jacob. *The Emergence of Judaism.* Louisville: Westminster John Knox Press, 2004.

Patterson, Richard D. "Joel." In *The Expositor's Bible Commentary,* vol. 7, edited by Frank E. Gaebelein. Grand Rapids, MI: Zondervan, 1985.

Pelikan, Jaroslav. *Whose Bible Is It? A History of the Scriptures Through the Ages.* New York: Viking Penguin, 2005.

Ray, Jr., Paul J. "The Duration of the Israelite Sojourn in Egypt." Bible and Spade 17, 2004.

Ryken, Philip. *The Love of Loves in the Song of Songs.* Wheaton, IL: Crossway, 2019.

Sailhamer, John H. "Genesis." In *The Expositor's Bible Commentary*, vol. 2, edited by Frank E. Gaebelein. Grand Rapids, MI: Zondervan, 1979.

Smick, Elmer B. "Job." In *The Expositor's Bible Commentary,* vol. 4, edited by Frank E. Gaebelein. Grand Rapids, MI: Zondervan, 1988.

Sweeney, Marvin A. "The Latter Prophets." In *The Hebrew Bible Today: An Introduction to Critical Issues,* edited by Steven L. McKenzie and Matt Patrick Graham. Louisville: Westminster John Knox Press, 1998.

Thiele, Edwin R. *The Mysterious Numbers of the Hebrew Kings.* Grand Rapids, MI: Eerdmans, 1965.

Thompson, J. A. *The Ancient Near Eastern Treaties and the Old Testament.* London: Tyndale, 1964.

VanGemeren, Willem A. "Psalms." In *The Expositor's Bible Commentary,* vol. 5, edited by Frank E. Gaebelein. Grand Rapids, MI: Zondervan, 1991.

Walton, John H. *Chronological and Background Charts of the Old Testament.* Grand Rapids, MI: Zondervan, 1994.

Weinreb, Tzvi Hersh and Joshua Schreier, eds. *Koren Talmud Bavli, The Noe Edition.* vol. *27: Tractate Bava Batra, Part One. Perek I Daf 15 Amud a.* Jerusalem: Koren, 2016.

Widder, Wendy L. "Daniel." In *The Story of God Bible Commentary,* edited by Tremper Longman III and Scot McKnight. Grand Rapids, MI: Zondervan, 2016.

Wolf, Herbert. "Judges." In *The Expositor's Bible Commentary,* vol. 3, edited by Frank E. Gaebelein. Grand Rapids, MI: Zondervan, 1992.

Wood, Leon J. "Hosea." In *The Expositor's Bible Commentary,* vol. 7, edited by Frank E. Gaebelein. Grand Rapids, MI: Zondervan, 1985.

Printed in the United States
by Baker & Taylor Publisher Services